TAKING TO THE ROAD

TAKING TO THE ROAD
MOTORCYCLING IN NEW ZEALAND

RHYS JONES

RANDOM HOUSE
NEW ZEALAND

For my late mother

ACKNOWLEDGEMENTS

Some of the photographs in this book are more than 25 years old. Although it has been difficult to identify some of the sources, every attempt has been made to do so. The following, however, can be credited for their contribution: Blue Wing Honda, The Perry family, The Munro family, The Bramwell family, Craig Roberts, Trevor Discombe, Rees Osborne, Dallas Alexander, Bernard Carpinter, Trevor Jones, Rod Coleman, Auckland War Memorial Museum, Krzysztof Pfeiffer, Ivor Evans, Elan Phillips, Yamaha, Kawasaki and Suzuki. A large proportion of the pictures are from the author's private collection.

National Library of New Zealand Cataloguing-in-Publication Data
Jones, Rhys.
Taking to the road : motorcycling in New Zealand / Rhys Jones.
Includes Index.
ISBN 1-86941-506-X
1. Motorcycles—New Zealand—History. 2. Motorcycles—New Zealand—
Pictorial works. 3. Motorcyclists—New Zealand. I. Title.
629.22750993—dc 21

A RANDOM HOUSE BOOK
published by
Random House New Zealand
18 Poland Road, Glenfield, Auckland, New Zealand

www.randomhouse.co.nz

First published 2002

© Rhys Jones 2002

The moral rights of the author have been asserted

ISBN 1 86941 506 X

Design: Dexter Fry
Layout: Graeme Leather
Cover design: Sharon Grace, Grace Design
Printed in China

Front cover: Honda's CB750. The first modern superbike, and one of the most significant models in the history of the motorcycle; BSA Gold Star. Simplicity and elegance. An icon of the British motorcycle industry; the author on Mike Hailwood's road-going Martini Yamaha in the Isle of Man, 1978; Aaron Slight on the V-4 Honda Superbike.

Back cover: Skimming the surf. A group of riders on Muriwai Beach, north of Auckland. The motorcycle at home in our environment.

CONTENTS

INTRODUCTION

Motorcyclists share a common bond. We all know what it's like to be cold and wet on a winter's morning, what it's like to be victimised by large four-wheeled vehicles, how it feels to hit a pothole or loose gravel when there's no warning sign on the road. All riders also know the feeling of achievement when these obstacles are overcome and know, too, the elation of taking off on a spring morning with the sun on our backs and the smell of freshly cut grass in our nostrils. And all motorcyclists know that exquisite feeling of freedom and independence on the road. If we all share common experiences as motorcyclists, as people we are more diverse than most groups with a common interest. This is what makes writing for motorcyclists such an enormous challenge.

I have spent most of my life close to motorcycles, either riding them or writing about them, and increasingly as the hair greys and the face wrinkles I ask myself the inevitable questions. Which period produced the best bikes, and when was motorcycling at its best? Was it the 1960s, '70s, '80s or '90s, is it right now, or was it a time that I didn't experience? The easiest part of the question is the bikes. Having ridden machines representing the past five decades, I have to say modern bikes are better to ride. They are safer, more reliable and the choice is greater than ever before. But it is not as simple as that. Every time I convince myself there's no time like the present, my thoughts drift back to the 1970s. I think of the sheer number of bikes on New Zealand roads then, the emergence in our showrooms of the great Japanese post-classic machines, the Marlboro Series, the revival of the Isle of Man, and the New Zealanders who went there. I remember riding Chas Mortimer's Isle of Man winning TZ250 at Ruapuna and negotiating gravel roads in the Waikato in the middle of the night in the Shell 500 24-Hour reliability trial. I also remember the Dunedin Festival road races on a circuit lined with kerbs, lampposts and brick walls. I will never forget the triumphs, the accidents, the wounds that were carried like trophies and the camaraderie of other riders.

I suppose it's easy to say that the selection of a favoured era will be dictated

The author on a 175cc Francis Barnett, from memory an underpowered but efficient and economical lightweight, in Christchurch around 1960. Riders had to remember to shake the bike in the morning as the oil would get to the bottom of the tank and foul the plug if it wasn't properly mixed with the petrol.

by the most cherished period in the life of whoever's doing the choosing, the period in which they had the most fun. I like to think my choice of the 1970s rests on more than personal experience. It is a simple fact that there were more motorcycles on New Zealand roads in the 1970s than at any other period before or since. There were more technological advances made than at any other time, and there was more emphasis on safety and protective clothing than at any previous time. Motorcycles became a much more acceptable, and respectable, form of transport and motorcycle sport reached a wider audience than ever before. Most of the initiatives that produced this state of affairs came from the Japanese, who spearheaded what amounted to a revolution in motorcycle design, manufacture and marketing. There is no question about it, the Japanese motorcycle revolution was the single most significant period in the 100-year history of motorcycling, and it hit New Zealand in the 1970s.

The author in 1976 on what some critics believe was the first Japanese bike to handle really well, a Suzuki GS1000. It was fast too, covering a standing quarter mile in 11.89s, with a terminal speed of 181.36kph. Only the Honda CBX and Yamaha's XS11 were quicker, and only by a whisker.

Having nominated what I believe to be the most important period for the motorcycle in this country I can't in all honesty isolate the 1970s for the purpose of this book. The Japanese revolution could not have taken place as it did without the ideas, ingenuity and pioneering efforts of the British, Americans and Europeans. The brilliant water-cooled two-strokes of the '70s were nothing new – the English company Scott had made a twin-cylinder two-stroke with water-cooled heads in 1913. It is common knowledge that Ernst Degner, an East German racer and engineer, defected to the West in 1961, taking all his two-stroke expertise to Suzuki. Soichiro Honda visited the Isle of Man TT races in 1954, and it's said he returned dejected to Japan because the European racing machinery was so much more advanced than Honda's. Twenty years later he returned to the island as the retiring president of the Honda Motor Company, the biggest motorcycle company in history.

I think it's important to view the 1970s in the context of the evolutionary process that followed the first crude attempts to motorise bicycles, and the extraordinary technology of the machines of today that have their roots in the '70s. To understand what happened in the 1970s it is necessary to look at the 1950s and '60s, when the seeds of the revolution were planted. Finally, a look at the 1980s and '90s is in order, to find the effects of the motorcycling revolution.

Throughout the first 100 years of the motorcycle, New Zealand has reflected trends in other parts of the world. New Zealand is in fact a microcosm of what has happened elsewhere. This book is not intended to be a definitive history of the motorcycle in New Zealand. More than anything else it is an attempt to trace the development of road and race bikes, and to capture some of the characters that have influenced motorcycling in this country. Many of them are racers, some are designers and engineers. Many of them have made their mark all over the world. They have assured New Zealand of a place in the world-wide web of motorcycling.

Rhys Jones

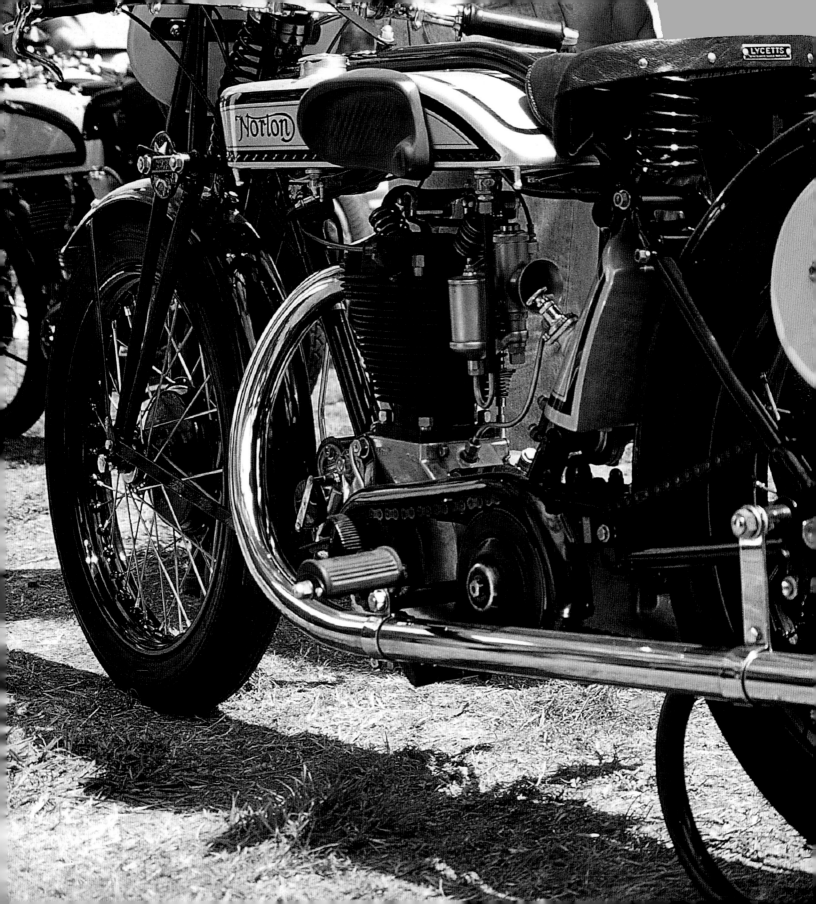

Chapter 1

GETTING STARTED

NEW Zealanders were introduced to the motorcycle in 1899 when a Christchurch resident by the name of Acton-Adams imported a $2\frac{1}{4}$ horsepower DeDion tricycle. The vehicle came from France where Albert DeDion and Georges Bouton had produced a machine that set the stage for the many motorcycle manufacturers who sprang up during the early part of the 20th century.

It is generally held that the DeDion was the first manufactured motorcycle, with manufactured the key word. French cycle maker Michaux had attached a steam engine to a bicycle as early 1869, fifteen years before Englishman Edward Butler reputedly built the first motorised tricycle. Then in 1885 German Gottlieb Daimler produced what many believe to be the first petrol driven motorcycle. But the Michaux, Butler and Daimler machines were

Is it, or is it not, a motorcycle? Although it bears little resemblance to the machines that have evolved since the beginning of the 20th century, this DeDion tricycle, imported by a Christchurch resident in 1899, is motor-driven, has a bicycle-type seat and handlebar steering – good enough to qualify it as the first motorcycle to be seen in New Zealand.

experimental and not manufactured in numbers. Without entering a debate about which marque can lay claim to being the very first motorcycle, it is fair to say that the DeDion was most definitely a front runner.

The first motorcycle to be made in New Zealand is a matter for conjecture. Cecil Wood from Timaru has been credited with being the first New Zealander to actually build a motorcycle, his machine running on the road for the first time in 1900. Others believe that S.W. Moult from Paraparaumu was first, with claims also being made for South Canterbury aviation pioneer Richard Pearse. When Moult retired in 1950, *NZ Motorcyclist* magazine said, 'He has seen the growth of motorcycling in New Zealand from its very earliest, and can very rightly be given the title of Father of New Zealand motorcycling.'

The convention of placing three- and two-wheel vehicles in the same category was established in the early days. The tricycle and bicycle were very similar . . . some believe the third wheel was merely for riders who couldn't stay upright on two. The four-stroke motor patented by DeDion and Bouton in 1889 was used in a tricycle because they considered a bicycle too unstable for their purpose. Most early motorcycles, whether two- or three-wheeled, were pedal cycles with engines attached. As the four-wheeled automobile developed so the tricycle gave way to two wheels. Sidecars would eventually bring three wheels back to favour, but these were never more than an attachment to a vehicle that was designed to run on two wheels. Once the car and the motorcycle were established there seemed little point in designers bothering themselves with three wheels.

Many of the New Zealanders who rushed to defend King and Country during the First World War saw the motorcycle, if not for the first time, in a completely different light. It was quickly recognised as an efficient way to deliver information. Radio was in its infancy and therefore unreliable and bikes

The Christchurch based NZ Motorcyclist *magazine recorded the events, bikes and personalities of the 1940s and '50s.*

became a vital means of communication on the Western Front. It was at this time that the term dispatch rider came into the language.

During the war the centre of motorcycle development shifted from Europe to the United States. The Americans pioneered such improvements as the twist-grip throttle control, rear drum brakes and the foot operated clutch. Many American motorcycles came to New Zealand after the war and in 1920 motorcycles from the United States outsold all others in New Zealand, probably for the first and only time.

It was during the boom years of the 1920s that the motorcycle began to reach a wider market in New Zealand and for a time during the decade there were more bikes than cars on the road. Increasingly they developed into an inexpensive means of transport for a young nation on the move. Bikes were put to use on the land as they handled rough terrain that would be off-limits to most cars of the day. American motorcycles such as the Indian and the

Percy Coleman, father of Rod and one of New Zealand's pioneer motorcycle racers. Most of his racing was on grass or dirt.

Harley-Davidson were popular, probably because they were built for similar frontier conditions. The distinction made today between on- and off-road machinery didn't exist then. Sealed roads were minimal and a rider could expect to face grass, gravel, mud or dust – and sometimes all four – on almost every journey.

The motorcycle also became a sporting vehicle, for as soon as any means of propulsion is invented someone will want to race it. Racing began on dirt and grass tracks and riders such as Percy Coleman rose to prominence. Reliability trials and economy trials were also popular throughout the 1920s and '30s. The Great Depression put the brakes on some of the recreational uses of the motorcycle but it didn't prevent a trickle of this newly found cheap transport finding its way to New Zealand.

As roads improved in the mid- to late 1930s, the more refined British machines took over and New Zealand motorcyclists had a choice of names such as BSA, Norton, AJS, Matchless, Triumph, Royal Enfield, Douglas, Velocette and Vincent.

Then, only 21 years after the end of the First World War, the motorcycle was called into military service again. Petrol was extremely hard to come by and in any case there were very few people left to ride the thirsty bikes. The Auckland Motorcycle Club's history *Seventy Five Years on Two Wheels* noted: 'By 1942 almost the whole male membership of the club was overseas. Of 108 financial members at the start of the war, only four were not in the armed services, all for health reasons.'

The war caused a temporory interruption to the British dominance when thousands of Indian motorcycles – part of a quarter of a million motorcycles the United States produced for a worldwide war effort – were brought here for the use of American troops. Many of these Army Indians have survived and are still running in New Zealand today.

Chapter 2

RULE BRITANNIA

During the immediate post-Second World War years, small inexpensive bikes provided transport primarily for people who couldn't afford cars. This advertisement emphasises the financial advantages of buying a BSA Bantam.

AFTER the Second World War the British dominance continued and most of the names that were familiar during the 1930s returned to New Zealand. Of newly registered bikes during September 1948, Triumph was top, followed closely by Royal Enfield and Ariel. The next four were Douglas, Matchless, AJS and BSA. Successful European bikes came later. Most were either German or Italian – having been on the losing side in the war, their manufacturing industries took some time to recover. When they did recover, the Italians in particular embraced new models and new ideas very quickly. Even so, it was difficult for the Europeans to make an impact in a country like New Zealand, with an essentially British heritage.

The decade and a half immediately after the war is the era regarded by many as the peak of British motorcycle development. The dominance enjoyed before the war may have been interrupted for five years but when civilian life resumed many of the models that survived were refined and reached their final stage of development. And although many motorcycle companies didn't survive the war, the ones that did looked good.

Many influential British classics are associated with the 1950s — bikes like the beautifully balanced BSA Gold Star, a simple and effective machine. It had a 499cc single-cylinder engine producing 40hp at 7000rpm. Weighing only 140kg in full sporting strip, it had a top speed of around 190kph. As well as the road version it was built in trial, scramble and racing versions. Another charismatic British marque, Triumph built the legendary Bonneville T120 in 1959. A 650cc parallel-twin with its roots in the 1938 Edward Turner Speed Twin, the Bonnie produced 46hp at 6500rpm and had a top speed of 180kph depending on the state of tune.

Forty years later the present day Triumph factory had so much faith in the original concept that they produced a new age Bonneville look-alike. Also in 1999, Kawasaki built a W650 air-cooled parallel twin that was as close to a Bonneville as you can get without putting the name on the side-covers. The success of these models is a testimony to the enduring popularity of the classic twin design.

Few British bikes of the period evoke such passion as the Vincent, originally called an HRD after the founder Howard R. Davies. The marque was sold to Philip Vincent, who produced a design that took other manufacturers years to match. In 1955 an un-supercharged 998cc Vincent Black Lightning reached a speed of 297.64kph in the hands of New Zealander Russell Wright in Christchurch – the only time that the two-wheeled land speed record left the northern hemisphere. Unfortunately Vincent closed its doors in the same year, but the big fast V-twin motor was prized in sporting circles for many years after.

Apart from the glamour machines, hundreds of small capacity bikes such as Francis Barnett, James and the BSA Bantam came here from Britain and all became familiar on New Zealand roads of the 1940s and '50s. Innumerable people started their motorcycling careers on BSA Bantams and it seems this simple little two-stroke, single-cylinder machine has now achieved cult status. The first Bantam appeared in 1946 and was manufactured with increasing refinement until 1971. During those 25 years the Bantam served novice riders, commuters, postal workers, off-road enthusiasts and road racers with distinction.

A not so successful lightweight came from Velocette, a manufacturer with a strong racing pedigree both before and immediately after the war. In 1948 they produced their controversial LE model – a 149cc flat-twin, with pressed steel monocoque body and water cooling, aimed obviously at commuters. In his 819 miles in three days road test for *NZ Motorcyclist* of November 1948, George Beresford wrote, 'I have covered similar distances at a higher speed, but never have I been carried on a motorcycle with more unassuming grace, with such charm of manner or with so slight a demand on my physical or mental powers.' In spite of George's enthusiasm, the LE was considered a failure and many believe it did much to bring the Velocette factory to its knees.

Many companies made what they assumed to be good business decisions by devoting money and energy to producing vehicles they believed would please a mass market. They may have been business decisions, but they weren't motorcycle decisions. The name Velocette has an unparalleled pedigree among motorcyclists, but to a commuter looking for a practical form of transport it

It's hard to believe that Len Perry went to the Isle of Man in 1939 and was on the race track at Pukekohe 60 years later. To call him durable is an understatement. He is one of the great characters of both racing and motorcycling in New Zealand.

LEN PERRY

Len Perry, a farmer's son, owned his first motorcycle at the age of fifteen in 1927. He first raced a year later at Hemming's Speedway at Mangere, where he logged up his first victory on a B4 AJS. Shortly afterwards came a new KDT Velocette, the first to arrive in New Zealand and a machine which took Perry to nineteen New Zealand titles. In all he won 42 national titles, a record unlikely to be surpassed. Like most of the riders of his era he raced on grass tracks as well as roads and dirt.

Perry and Henry Fletcher laid out the first New Zealand TT circuit on Waiheke Island in 1932. He first rode in the Isle of Man in 1939, a few months before the Second World War broke out. Back home he had five years in the Air Force before things got back to normal. It was during the immediate post-war period that Perry enjoyed his most successful run, winning seven New Zealand TT races. Such was his ability to ride bikes of any kind, he also won the national solo speedway title and in 1947 captained the New Zealand test team that toured Australia.

Len Perry spent the majority of his career riding in New Zealand. This was probably because, when he was in his prime, competing overseas was an expensive and time-consuming occupation. He also lost five years, from the ages of 27 to 32, to the war. He was chosen to represent New Zealand at the Isle of Man eight times, but managed only three visits, the last in 1951. He allegedly had his last race in 1974, but couldn't be kept away from the track. In 1999, at the age of 87, he rode several laps of honour at Pukekohe with the great Giacomo Agostini. In 2002 Len raced again at Pukekohe at the age of 90, which must be some kind of a record.

Riding without a helmet was to cease at the beginning of the 1970s. Although many riders were voluntarily wearing safety helmets, there were some who objected to the compulsory helmet law, preferring the wind in their hair.

careless
OVERTAKERS
are
good

business
for
UNDERTAKERS

Be careful when overtaking !

ISSUED BY THE TRANSPORT DEPARTMENT

Vulnerability on the road has always been an issue with motorcyclists, this 1950s Transport Department advertisement emphasising the dangers of unwise overtaking. Interestingly, New Zealand has double the number of bikes on the road today and 30 per cent fewer accidents.

meant nothing. Probably the worst examples of this can be found in the British car industry. Many will remember the charismatic MG badge being attached to Austin 1100s and various other mass-market cars. In a logical reaction, MG enthusiasts sneered and shunned the cars and the mass-market buyers didn't care what their vehicle was called as long as it served its purpose at the right price.

Throughout the 1950s the motorcycling status quo continued. But towards the end of the decade the great British factories were providing bikes for a shrinking market. The post-war scooter boom was beginning to wane, the result of more and more people being able to afford cars and the two-wheeled industry was heading for the doldrums.

Above

The British police liked them, but the Velocette LE is generally considered a folly by a factory that should have known better.

Right

Another of the British classic marques whose machines came to New Zealand before and after the Second World War, Ariel began production of motorcycles in 1902 and continued until 1970. The bike pictured is a single cylinder OHV 350cc Red Hunter, made in 1953.

Left

A very simple single-cylinder two-stroke machine, the BSA Bantam was meant to achieve immediately after the Second World War what the Honda step-thru managed to do in the 1960s.

Below

A 1956 single cylinder 500cc Matchless, a simple and elegant motorcycle, popular in New Zealand and representative of one of Britain's oldest marques. The company started in 1899 and survived in one form or another until 1969. A 432cc Matchless ridden by Charlie Collier won the first Isle of Man TT in 1907.

One of the most charismatic of all British marques, the Vincent was best known for its big V-twin motors, but the factory also made a single, before and after the Second World War. Called the Comet, it had a 499cc engine. It was in fact the V-twin motor with the rear cylinder removed. This is a 1951 model.

A very well cared for 750 Norton Commando at an Auckland race meeting. The single disc at the front suggests that it is an early 1970s model.

The Triumph Trident, with a five-speed gearbox and a 740cc motor, was one of the last attempts to save the British motorcycle industry. Although the triple-cylinder engine was fast enough and the bike was successful on the race track, it couldn't stem the Japanese tide. Those which have survived, like this one, are prized.

A well looked after 1958 Triumph Tiger 100. Many pre-1960s machines have made their way into museums or the private garages of collectors and are rarely started. Others, like this one, are used regularly in classic rides and rallies.

Opposite above

Although the last Manx was built by Norton in 1962, such is the fascination with the model, one of the best known and most successful racing machines of all time, it is still possible to fill a racing grid with Manx Nortons in New Zealand to this very day. Now that bike builders like Ken McIntosh are making the bikes, it is likely the single-cylinder 350cc and 500cc racers will dominate classic racing fields for as long as people race motorcycles. The bike pictured is a 1962 348cc model.

Opposite below

AJS 7R. Built as a 350 and a 500, the 7R was, apart from the Manx Norton, the best known of British racing motorcycles and the machine Rod Coleman rode in the early 1950s during his years as a works rider. Known as the 'boy racer', the 7R is, like the Manx, now being built in replica form for classic racing. This is a 1951 350 single.

Above

Velocette Thruxton. Perhaps the ultimate example of a superbly engineered sporting British motorcycle, the Thruxton, a 499cc single producing 41hp, was named for the English race track of the same name. It is ironic that such a handsome machine, now much sought after by collectors, should be produced in 1970 as the lights were being switched off in the motorcycle industry all over Britain.

Chapter 3

KIWIS AND THE ISLE OF MAN

IN 1914, just before the outbreak of the First World War, Alex Anderson became the first New Zealander to ride at the Isle of Man, beginning a love affair between Kiwi riders and the island's Tourist Trophy races that has continued to the present day. It isn't by accident that the first New Zealand TT races, in 1931, were held on Waiheke; the Hauraki Gulf island being chosen because of its similarity to the Isle of Man – a rural island lying a relatively short sea journey from a major population base. The races were held on Waiheke until war brought them to a halt in 1942. They resumed in 1945 and remained there until 1950. In most years the winner on Waiheke would be sponsored to the Isle of Man – the motorcycling equivalent of being chosen for the All Blacks.

Racing had started on the Isle of Man, in the middle of the Irish sea, in 1907, the island being chosen because authorities wouldn't allow public roads to be closed for racing anywhere else in Great Britain. The Mecca for motorcycle road racing enthusiasts from all over the world, the Isle of Man virtually always saw New Zealanders in attendance, but this country's first success wasn't achieved until 1954 when Rod Coleman, the most successful

In one of the most celebrated comebacks in sporting history, Mike Hailwood celebrates winning the 1978 TT Formula One race, and with it his tenth world championship, on the Isle of Man. Second-placed John Williams stands next to him.

Kiwi road racer of the 1950s, won the 350cc Junior TT. New Zealand's tally of Isle of Man victories between 1954 and 2002 is headed by Graeme Crosby with three, Hugh Anderson two, and Rod Coleman, Dennis Ireland, Robert Holden, Brett Richmond and Bruce Anstey with one each.

No doubt our fascination with the Isle of Man was a huge factor in street racing becoming a great Kiwi tradition with Cust, Halswell, Mangere, Taumarunui, Wanganui, Gisborne, Whakatane, Paeroa, Te Aroha, Gracefield and Manukau among venues here. In the 1970s the Ceramco Grand Prix was run in the streets of Auckland and the Festival race in the streets of Dunedin. As purpose-built race tracks are expensive and the often-used airfields featureless and lacking excitement, street racing is pivotal in the history of motorcycle racing in this country.

The shift away from street racing in most countries began in the 1960s but didn't really bite until the Isle of Man lost its World Championship status in 1976. The great Giacomo Agostini, after many brilliant victories on the island, saying in 1972 that he would never ride there again was a telling blow. The coming of slick tyres and machines that bore no resemblance, especially in performance, to road bikes made the street races increasingly dangerous.

Street races in New Zealand have probably survived because the bulk of our racing is undertaken with machines that are basically modified road bikes. We have seen the odd superbike in recent years, but even they have a road bike base. We haven't, however, seen a pukka 500cc Grand Prix racing machine, with the exception of the experimental BSL, on our street circuits for many years.

Whether street circuits will survive is the subject of fierce debate. They are certainly healthy in New Zealand but only as long as the authorities deem them to be safe . . . which means as long as the level of injury sustained by riders and, especially, spectators is kept to an acceptable level. It could be that

Programme for the Isle of Man TT in 1977, the year that multiple world champion Phil Read returned to the island for a reported large sum of money after previously boycotting the island course saying it was too dangerous. The TT Formula One World Championship, consisting of a one-off five-lap race, was introduced in 1977, the authorities believing it would bring back some credibility after the races lost their Grand Prix World Championship status.

Crosby first served notice to the international scene in the Marlboro Series. Here he lifts the front wheel of the road based Kawasaki Z1 in the company of Stu Avant 1, John Woodley 6, and Warren Willing W, all riding Grand Prix machinery.

GRAEME CROSBY

Graeme Crosby will be remembered as one of the last of that breed of motorcyclists who could, and did, ride just about anything. Today, with sponsorship and contractual obligations confining the top riders to very narrow boundaries, the degree of specialisation is such that this can no longer happen. It is true that Crosby achieved only second in the 500cc World Championship, but as well as mastering the billiard table smooth GP circuits, he was victorious on the treacherous street circuits of Northern Island and the Isle of Man as well as here in New Zealand. He conquered the spectacular speed bowl at Daytona and the pressure cooker of Suzuka.

He came away with two world championships in Formula One, the forerunner of today's Superbikes.

Crosby won the Senior TT on the Isle of Man in 1980 in only his second year on the island – the first New Zealander to win the Senior TT in 73 years of trying – and in Australia brought the big works four-stroke Suzuki to the Swann Series and cleaned up. Earlier, the first signs of his brilliance had been evident in every round of the final Marlboro Series before he moved overseas and there can be little doubt that Crosby left the international scene too soon. Many believe that he was still on the way up when he returned to New Zealand.

HUGH ANDERSON

Hugh Anderson is one of the most outstanding racers produced by New Zealand. Born in Auckland in 1936, he enjoyed success both on and off road before leaving for Europe and the Isle of Man in 1960 with an AJS 7R and Manx Norton. In 1961 he crashed heavily and, like the clouds with a silver lining story, married the Dutch nurse who was caring for him. His fortunes then picked up and he was signed by Suzuki, the factory that gave him his greatest Grand Prix successes from 1963 to 1965. Riding the remarkable little two-stroke machines in the lightweight classes, he was double world champion in 1963 in the 50cc and 125cc class. He won the 50cc world title again in 1964 and the 125cc in 1965. He was third in the 125cc class in 1964 and in the 50cc class in 1965. Anderson won eight 50cc and seventeen 125cc Grand Prix. No other New Zealander, and only one Australian, Mick Doohan, has bettered Anderson's 25 Grand Prix victories.

Anderson first rode at the Isle of Man TT in 1960 on the Norton. His record on the island for the 1963 to '66 seasons is: 1963, winner Lightweight 125cc TT and runner up Lightweight 50cc TT; 1964, winner of Lightweight 50cc TT; 1965, fifth Lightweight 125cc and runner-up Lightweight 50cc TT; 1966, third in Lightweight 125cc and Lightweight 50cc TTs.

Since his retirement from the Grand Prix scene, Anderson has played an active part in classic racing and has competed, primarily on Manx Nortons, all over the world. He regularly turns out for classic meetings in New Zealand. Anderson has remained competitive into his 60s and beat Barry Sheene, sixteen years his junior, in a classic race in Australia in 2000.

Hugh Anderson is seen here on board one of Giacomo Agostini's MV Agustas at Pukekohe in 1999.

the sport's administrators will decide that street circuits will be confined to Classic bikes and the increasingly popular Post-Classic bikes from the 1970s. This would be one way of putting a cap on spiralling speeds and concerns about the corresponding danger to riders and spectators.

To use one example, a 500cc Manx Norton, perhaps the most charismatic British racing machine of the immediate pre- and post-war period, produced around 50 horsepower. Today just about any motorcycle dealer will have sports machines on the showroom floor generating over 100 horsepower. As for race bikes, in 1972 Kawasaki and Honda produced 100hp machines that were shredding rear tyres. When the tyre technology caught up, the power increased again and today 500cc Grand Prix bikes have around double that horsepower. Top speed of these machines is over 300kph. Even 250cc Grand Prix race bikes are reaching speeds of up to 270kph.

American Pat Hennen, three times a winner of the New Zealand Marlboro Series, was one of the last non-British Grand Prix riders to race on the Isle of Man, in 1978 suffering a hideous crash there that ended his racing career.

The *Motocourse Annual* of 1978/79 said of the 1978 TT: 'Five dead, countless bumps, abrasions and fractures, plus an American brain [Hennen] rattled to all-hell-and-back just isn't on these days. Voluntary it may be; lethal it most definitely is. The TT will go the way Rolls-Royce did. And even that was unthinkable.'

Unthinkable it may be, but the Isle of Man TT is still a British tradition going strong and doesn't even look like going the way of Rolls-Royce. Hundreds of riders and thousands of spectators flock to the island every June, just as they have since 1907, with New Zealanders providing the largest non-British contingent.

As well as Pat Hennen and its home-grown riders, New Zealand has a strong 1970s connection to the Isle of Man through the deeds of Mike Hailwood, generally acknowledged as the greatest road racer of all time.

Apart from the occasional celebrity ride, Mike had pulled out of World Championship racing, having won nine titles, in 1969. He'd then turned to cars, winning the 1972 European Formula Two Championship in a

ROD COLEMAN

New Zealand's first Grand Prix World Championship works rider, Coleman led the AJS works team in 1953 and '54, in the second season winning the Isle of Man Junior 350cc TT and the Swedish 500cc Grand Prix. Coleman's Isle of Man victory tends to overshadow his many other achievements, as the IOM was the pinnacle of road race accomplishment at the time. His record in Europe during the first four seasons in the '50s is impressive as during this time he was riding against a Norton team which at various times included Geoff Duke, Reg Armstrong, Ray Amm and Jack Brett. It was a time when the Italian challenge was beginning with Bill Lomas and Les Graham riding MV Agustas and Umberto Massetti a Gilera-4 and Fergus Anderson a Moto Guzzi.

Not surprisingly Coleman was nearly unbeatable on New Zealand circuits. He also cleaned up at Bathurst in 1954, winning the Australian 350 and 500 TTs. Rod and his brother Bob, who raced with distinction in New Zealand and Ireland, consolidated a motorcycle dynasty begun in the 1920s by their father Percy. All astute businessmen, they built a motorcycle dealership known to anyone in New Zealand with even a fleeting association with motorcycling.

Surtees-Ford, raced in Formula One for Surtees in 1973, then joined McLaren in 1974. He was awarded the George Medal for bravery when he risked his life to drag Clay Regazoni from the burning wreck of his car in the South African Grand Prix. Following a serious injury sustained in a Formula One crash at the Nurburgring, Hailwood retired from motor sport and moved from South Africa to Auckland.

To begin with Mike Hailwood lived a relaxing and uneventful life in New Zealand. He maintained close links with the motorcycle community, and many afternoons were spent around his swimming pool in the company of Stuart Avant, Graeme Crosby and other young riders with an eye on a European future.

Hailwood's return to the Isle of Man was prompted when Phil Read, who had pulled out of racing on the island, vowing never to return, had gone back and won. Hailwood's attitude was: 'If he can do it so can I.' But in the year of his decision, 1977, Hailwood was 37 years old and hadn't raced on the Isle of Man since 1967 – he hadn't raced any sort of bike since 1971.

When the British media got hold of the fact that he was to return to the Isle of Man TT things began to happen. Sports Motorcycles in Manchester signed

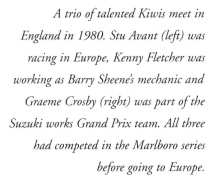

A trio of talented Kiwis meet in England in 1980. Stu Avant (left) was racing in Europe, Kenny Fletcher was working as Barry Sheene's mechanic and Graeme Crosby (right) was part of the Suzuki works Grand Prix team. All three had competed in the Marlboro series before going to Europe.

him to ride a 900cc Ducati in the Formula One race and drinks manufacturer Martini announced that they would sponsor him on works 250cc and 500cc two-stroke Yamahas. As Mike had no experience of the new breed of two-strokes, his preliminary preparation was conducted at Pukekohe where Bob Haldane dutifully took his TZ700 on many afternoons.

Not having raced a bike for six years, Hailwood had only three races before returning to the island. He rode a Ducati in the Australian Six-Hour race with Jim Scaysbrook, a TZ750 at Bathurst and a 750 Ducati, again with Scaysbrook, at the Adelaide Three-Hour.

Hailwood's Isle of Man victory came in the TT Formula One race on the Ducati. It was a glorious sunny afternoon with a massive crowd cheering him on. The victory gave him his tenth and final World Championship.

Hailwood returned to New Zealand briefly, during which time he raced a 350cc AJS to fourth place in a classic race at Wigram near Christchurch. To my knowledge this was the only time he raced a bike in New Zealand. In 1979 he returned to the Isle of Man and won the 500cc Senior TT on a two-stroke Suzuki Grand Prix machine. He had one more race at Mallory Park, and one more crash, in which he shattered his collarbone. Then he retired just short of his fortieth birthday.

Eighteen months later Michael Stanley Bailey Hailwood, MBE GM, and his daughter Michelle died following a car accident in England. With 76 Grand Prix victories and ten World Championships to his credit, it was a shocking way to go. At the end of the 20th century three polls were mounted to find the greatest rider of the previous 100 years. Magazine editors and their readers around the world, together with the current Grand Prix and Superbike riders, were asked to vote. All three groups voted Hailwood first, and by massive margins. Bear in mind that it's doubtful that any of the present crop of riders would have even seen him race. The accolade legend is often overused and seldom applied to the real thing. Hailwood, like only a handful of other sportsmen, remains a true legend. All those who were close to motorcycles in New Zealand in the 1970s will remember him fondly.

Another of the last generation of riders who could ride anywhere, Pat Hennen mastered the twisting street and short circuits of New Zealand, the smooth European Grand Prix circuits and the Isle of Man. It was, however, the Isle of Man that brought his promising career to an early end.

Douglas in the Isle of Man during race week. The Victorian buildings of this conservative seaside town provide an unlikely backdrop for the thousands of motorcyclists who flock to the island every June for the TT races.

The author with Mike Hailwood (centre) and Graeme Crosby (right) at the Isle of Man in 1980. Hailwood had won the Senior 500cc TT in 1979, Crosby would win it in 1980 and go on to win two other classes in 1981. This shot was taken just before the start of the rain delayed Senior race.

Graeme Crosby doesn't believe in wasting champagne in the usual manner. Flanked by runner-up Steve Cull on the left and third-placed Steve Ward on the right, he swigs from the bottle after becoming, in 1980, the first Kiwi to win the Isle of Man Senior TT. All three placegetters rode Suzuki Grand Prix bikes. And there are no umbrella girls here, just a couple of boy scouts, the youth organisation having operated the manual leader board at the races since the very early days of the TT.

Graeme Crosby in the pits after his winning ride at the 1980 Isle of Man TT. He had a natural ability that made him hard to beat on the island but he later expressed concerns about safety there.

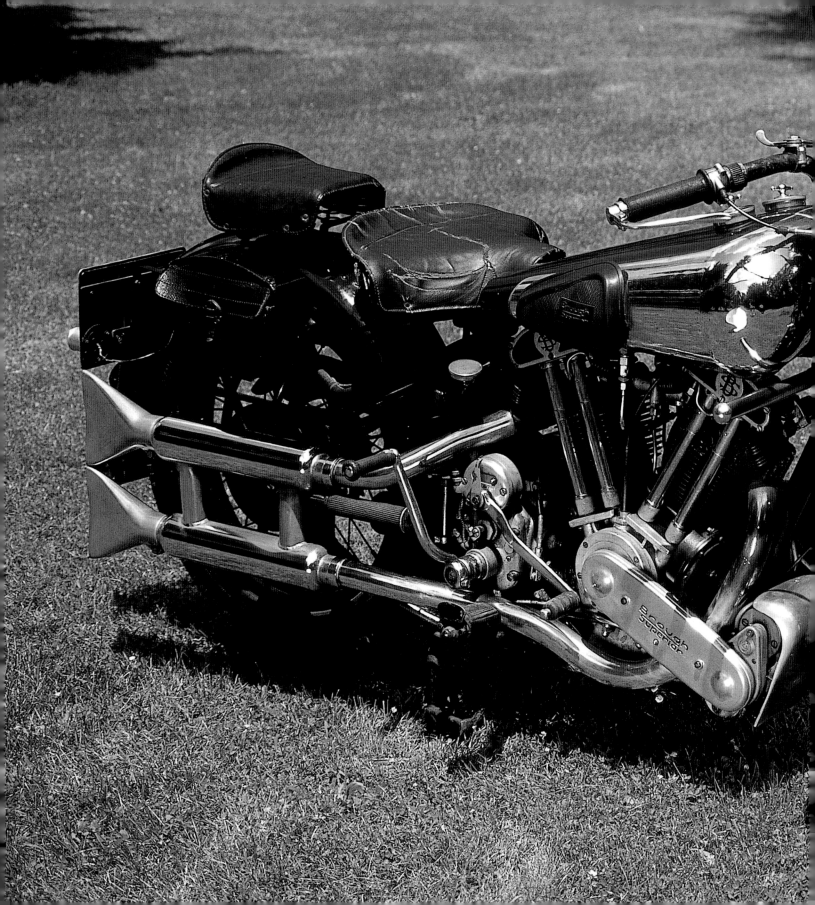

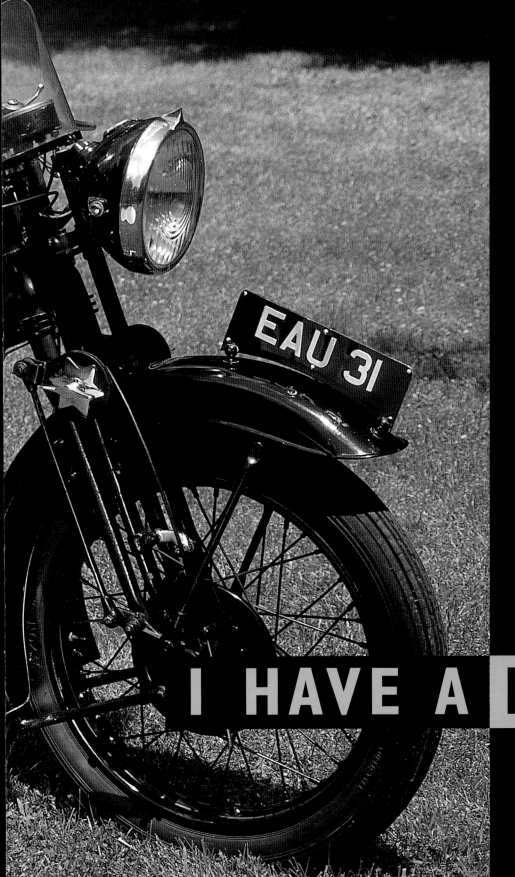

EAU 31

Chapter 4

I HAVE A DREAM

IN the 1960s something happened that wasn't confined to motorcycles – it happened with electronics, photography, home appliances and the motor industry in general. Japan shook off the devastating effects of the Second World War, quicker it seems than some of the victors in that conflict, and became an economic powerhouse. No longer were they producing cheap copies of Western goods; they had learned quickly how to absorb ideas and improve on them.

Their greatest achievement was to make consumer goods affordable to a mass market. The simple premise that it is more profitable to sell 3000 inexpensive motorcycles than 300 expensive ones only applies if the manufacturer can make them efficiently. The post-war Japanese demonstrated how to do it on a grand scale. They were soon to become the second-biggest economy in the world and the largest producer of motorcycles ever.

When the 1960s dawned, the first stirrings of the Japanese age of motor-cycling became evident. At London's Earls Court Motorcycle Show of 1960 more than 50 manufacturers, representing twelve different countries, displayed their motorcycles, scooters and sidecars. One of them, Honda, showed just three models, a 125cc Benly, a Benly Super Sport and a 247cc Dream – the Dream featuring an electric starter and indicators. Many were impressed, some sceptical.

What happened over the next 20 years amounted to a transport revolution as the Japanese drove the biggest sales boom in the 100-year history of the motorcycle. The man at the helm was Soichiro Honda, whose achievements in the transportation industry have been compared to those of Henry Ford. The story goes that after the Second World War, with most of Japan in ruins and the people suffering dreadful shortages of basic necessities, Honda was given a 50cc engine. He fitted the little motor to his bicycle and for a fuel tank attached a water bottle – filled with oil extracted from the roots of pine trees because of a petrol shortage. As only 500 of the engines were available he decided to make his own . . . and so, in 1948, the Honda Motor Company was established.

One of Soichiro Honda's ambitions was to have his machines win the Isle of

Man TT. In 1959, when Honda sent a race team to the island for the first time, many Europeans laughed. The Hondas filled sixth, seventh and eighth positions in the 125cc class. Two years later they filled the first five places in the 125cc TT and the first five in the 250cc TT. They also filled the first five places in the 1961 250cc World Championship – a remarkable achievement. The laughing had stopped.

If the British and European motorcycle industries thought they could cope with Honda, there was more bad news to come. Yamaha, a company which began making musical organs in the 19th century, started to take an interest in motorcycle manufacture in 1953. In honour of the company's founder, Taraguchi Yamaha, a tuning fork was used as the company logo and remains as a reminder of that musical heritage on Yamaha motorcycles even today.

Soichiro Honda, founder of the biggest motorcycle company in the world. He was a man with dreams, and they all came true. He played an important role in the history of transportation.

Around the same time that Yamaha were developing their first motorcycle, a manufacturer of wooden weaving looms called Suzuki had also recognised the opportunities for motorcycle manufacture. The fourth major Japanese name arose from a combination of two brands, Meihatsu and Meguro. They joined forces under the banner of the industrial giant Kawasaki, whose aircraft division had also recognised the growing demand for motorcycles.

Other Japanese brands, among them Lilac, Tohatsu and Bridgestone, emerged in the 1950s but few were exporters and by the 1960s the four major companies emerged as market leaders in Japan. These four factories would completely dominate the entire motorcycle world with around 80 per cent of all motorcycles in existence today having been put together in a Japanese factory. In 1969 Japan produced 2,570,000 motorcycles and Britain produced 71,000. In 1975 the Japanese were producing 3,800,000 machines and Britain 40,000.

How the use of attractive women to sell motorcycles has changed. This conservative pose, taken in 1970, looks almost Victorian when compared with some of the raunchy photography in many magazines today.

Although the 1970s was the period in which the Japanese motorcycle industry buried the Europeans almost completely, it was the 1960s when the guard began to change. One highly visible example late in the decade was the way our universities came to be surrounded by hundreds of inexpensive, small-capacity Japanese motorcycles. At the same time the Honda step-thru, which had effectively transferred millions of Asians from bicycles to motorcycles and made a significant contribution to cheap and efficient transport all over the world, became one of the most common sights on New Zealand roads.

In the early 1960s the Japanese concentrated on small capacity machines, for the time being leaving the big bike market to the British. In some ways this was an advantage for the British manufacturers. Because of the abundance of inexpensive small Japanese bikes coming into the market, more people began to ride, and when they wanted to move up to something more powerful they swapped their 125cc or 300cc for a 650cc Triumph or Norton.

Bill White, Mayor of Newmarket and motorcycle enthusiast, ran the successful Auckland dealership W. White's, a company behind many of the production and race bikes on the tracks in the 1970s.

This cosy evolutionary accident didn't last long. The Japanese were about to enact the final sequence in the domination of the world's motorcycle markets.

With only a flicker of resistance the Europeans had surrendered the small bike and commuter market but in the mid-1960s, when the Japanese began to turn their attention to the bigger bikes, they found the battle not quite so easy. There was still some life among the large capacity European bikes at the end of the 1960s and Norton, Triumph and BSA enjoyed some success in their home and overseas markets. Models like the Norton Commando and Triumph's Bonneville carried the flag into the next decade but they carried with them 1960s and sometimes '50s technology.

New Zealand importers who had been dependent on mainly British machinery quickly introduced Japanese brands into their stables. At W. White's showroom in Newmarket a gleaming range of Yamahas jostled for floor space with trusty Triumphs while Suzukis began to fight for space with Nortons at Bill Russell's. The buzz of what some called Japanese sewing machine engines could be heard everywhere. The word on the shop floor was that the large capacity, oil-leaking dinosaurs were finished. Smaller capacity, high-revving machines were cheaper, more efficient and faster. This turned out to be partially true, but only at a certain stage.

BURT MUNRO

Burt Munro defies category – sportsman, engineer, inventor, home mechanic, great eccentric, he answers to them all and there has never been anything quite like him in New Zealand motorcycling.

His introduction came when he bought an Indian Scout for transport in 1920 and five years later he began to turn his attention to competitive riding with grass- and dirt-track racing, speedway and hill climbs. When an accident in the early 1940s saw him lose his job, he decided to devote his life to the development of his Indian. In the 1960s Munro made his first trip to Bonneville Salt Flats in Utah to launch an assault on an AMA world speed record. In all, he made the trip fourteen times, lifted a couple of class records, and became the rider of the world's fastest Indian at 191.34mph (306.14kph). Between his trips to the United States, Munro worked in his garage in Invercargill where he tuned the same engine for 50 years. In the garage were his bed, a lathe and a pot-bellied stove for forging. The stove was also used for winter heating and cooking. Perhaps the most important ingredient in that garage was the enormous spirit and determination of Burt Munro. He was still working on the bike when he died in 1978.

The Japanese factories, cautious as ever, moved from the small-capacity bikes into middleweights. They intended to dominate all classes, but one at a time. Honda's CB450 four-stroke and the quick 250 and 350 two-strokes from Yamaha and Suzuki began to set the pace with the two-stroke middleweights outperforming most of the British big bikes.

In 1968 Suzuki increased the pace of change again. A two-stroke 500cc twin called the T500 was regarded as the first Japanese big bike, proving to be fast and reliable. It was a popular engine with the racing fraternity as well as road riders and in 1971 New Zealander Keith Turner used the Suzuki twin to claim second position in the 500cc World Championship. Such was the speed of Japanese development that the mantle of top Japanese big bike remained with the Suzuki T500 for less than a year. Although it was produced until 1972, the big, by the standards of the time, Suzuki was overshadowed by the first two big bikes, or superbikes of the modern era, the Honda CB750 and the Kawasaki 500 Mach 3.

The domination of the small bike market was mirrored in racing. Mike Hailwood had given the Japanese their first World Championship on a 250cc Honda in 1961. The following year they took out the 350cc, 250cc, 125cc and 50cc World Championships. In 1963 New Zealander Hugh Anderson won two of his four World Championships on 50cc and 125cc Suzukis. From then on it was a rapid downhill ride for the European brands. From 1962 to '67 the Japanese won every World Championship except the 500cc class. That's 24 championships in six years.

It wasn't until 1975 that the last bastion of European dominance, the 500cc class, fell to the Japanese. Ironically it was Giacomo Agostini, who had won seven 500cc championships on an Italian MV Agusta, who gave the Japanese their first title in the big bike class. In another milestone, the Yamaha he rode was the first two-stroke to win the class. Following that victory a Japanese four-cylinder two-stroke motorcycle has won every 500cc World Championship since.

After 52 years the 500cc class came to an end in 2001, providing a most extraordinary statistic. The first 26 titles were won by European manufacturers, the last 26 by Japanese – surely one of the neatest and most telling statistics in all motorcycle sport.

At the end of the 1960s and into the early '70s, in spite of the Japanese onslaught, many motorcyclists who could afford bigger bikes stuck with the British marques. Triumph and BSA, who were by then part of the same group, launched a three-cylinder 750cc motor to power the Triumph Tridents and BSA Rockets. The bikes were successful on the racetrack and regarded as very prestigious motorcycles but they couldn't hold back the tide for long.

Rod Coleman made the following observation: 'Apart from the Triumph motorcycle factory the rest of the industry were not marketers in the overseas market. They were merely order takers in these markets and concentrated their marketing in Britain. Even when the Japanese began to make motorcycles socially acceptable it still took the British factories too long to react. The horse had already bolted by the time they tried to compete against the Japanese.

'Even then they got their priorities the wrong way round. For instance, when I attended the grand opening of the very large and palatial new BSA and Triumph headquarters at Duarte in California in 1966, I did not see anything in the model range which was going to help them get back on top. What I did see, only a few miles away, were the headquarters for Honda, Suzuki and Yamaha which were only about half the size of the new BSA Triumph headquarters but which were fully stocked and selling very quickly the type of motorcycle which the public wanted.'

The Yamaha XS1100. The competition was getting tougher for the Europeans when Yamaha's 95hp XS1100 appeared on the scene in 1977. The XS weighed in at a hefty 256kg, but this, its followers said, gave it exceptional stability at high touring speeds and the smooth four-cylinder 1100cc shaft-driven bike was described as a long distance rider's dream come true.

The Honda VF750S. While the major Japanese players were developing their in-line four-cylinder four-strokes, Honda began in the early 1980s the development of a V-four. The engine would eventually appear in Superbike race bikes and in the enduring and very popular VFR800.

Chapter 5

YOU MEET THE NICEST PEOPLE ON A HONDA

IN 1973 BSA, who had made their first motorcycle in 1909, reached the end of a long road. Triumph staggered on through the 1970s, bogged by industrial problems and bad management, kept alive, in all probability, by a handful of enthusiasts. The factory introduced an electric start on the Trident in 1974 but by 1976 it was all over and the last batch of Tridents were sold to the Saudi Arabian Police Force. On the verge of bankruptcy, Norton in 1975 desperately introduced an electric starter and full range of accessories for the Commando. But the engine was outdated in 1973 and the bike lasted only until 1977. It would take more than an electric start to compete with the might of Japan. With the three remaining British bikes out of the race, the Japanese had all but won the motorcycling war.

It would be another 20 years before the Europeans showed any real evidence of recovery. The last sign of European defiance in the early 1970s came from Japan's war-time allies Italy and Germany. The Italian company Ducati produced the first of a long and successful line of sporting desmodromic 90 degree V-twins and Germany's BMW a range of durable boxer twins. The 899cc BMW R90S, with 67 bhp and a top speed of 200kph, found a ready market and the beautiful Ducati 750 Sport of 1973 and 900 Super Sport of 1974 won dedicated support. But, compared with the Japanese, they were capturing only niche markets; aristocrats overwhelmed by the voice of the people. There was a massive motorcycle market out there, calling for fast, reliable and stylish motorcycles and at a reasonable price. Honda, Kawasaki, Suzuki and Yamaha were delivering the goods.

When Honda struck the first blow in the battle for the big bike market, they knew the real showdown was with the other Japanese factories. Not only did they start the modern superbike era but they did it with an engine configuration that eventually became the backbone of the whole Japanese industry – the in-line four-cylinder four-stroke. The bike was the CB750.

Kawasaki, apparently working on a similar project, were said to be stunned and took three years to respond. In 1972 they threw down the gauntlet with the mighty 900Z1. It wasn't simply a larger capacity in-line four; it was a different motorcycle. Kawasaki didn't copy Honda, they made their own

The New Zealand Motorcycle *flourished in the 1970s as importers realised the need to advertise in an increasingly competitive environment.*

version. Although the Z1 probably won the battle for superbike supremacy at the time, Honda must be given credit for getting there first.

At the end of the decade, Honda and Kawasaki went head to head again. This time they produced a couple of monsters. The six-cylinder Honda CBX, inspired by the factory's six-cylinder race bikes of the 1960s, came first. Kawasaki also produced six-cylinders in the form of the Z1300. The CBX was air-cooled, had 24 valves and six carburettors. The engine looked huge but at 260kg it weighed less than the CB750. With 105bhp on tap it was the first road bike to top the magical 100bhp.

The Kawasaki Z1300 had less of a sporting nature than the CBX. It was shaft driven, weighed 320kg, and was water-cooled, but it did produce 120bhp to help shift the extra bulk. Like the big bikes that opened the 1970s, both the even bigger sixes have achieved cult status, and it's unlikely that anything quite like them will be built again.

To begin with, Yamaha and Suzuki took different lines. Suzuki launched the GT750, a three-cylinder, water-cooled two-stroke, known affectionately as

'You Meet the Nicest People on a Honda' . . . an advertising slogan which became synonymous with the rise in popularity of the small, clean and efficient motorcycles that poured out of the Japanese factories in the 1960s and '70s.

the 'water bottle'. Yamaha seemed content with the huge success of the RD250 and 350 two-stroke range. When they decided it was time for a big bore four-stroke they chose the three-cylinder XS750. Suzuki made another radical move by introducing the rotary engined RE5. Suzuki had a contract with inventor Felix Wankel and the German company NSU to produce the motors, but the project was deemed a commercial failure and eventually dropped.

In retrospect, although the 1970s produced an unprecedented array of exotic and radical machinery, by the beginning of the 1980s all the big four factories were firmly in the in-line, four-cylinder, four-stroke camp.

The immediate effect of the Japanese motorcycle revolution was obvious. More people could get around and for less money. Cars in New Zealand in the 1960s and '70s were among the most expensive in the world. Unlike today, cars were out of reach of all but a few students and certainly totally out of the wildest dreams of high-school pupils. The bulk of small and medium motorcycle buyers were young and bikes gave them a new-found freedom and independence. Many would ride bikes only until they could afford cars but nevertheless they had learned to ride and had been exposed to motorcycling. Many of these riders began to return to motorcycling in their 30s, 40s and 50s. They returned not to find cheap transport but to capture the thrill of riding a bike again.

Another noticeable effect was that the Japanese did much to make motorcycling more socially acceptable. Many New Zealanders, who had never been exposed to motorcycling, regarded anybody riding a bike as a potential bike gang member. The prejudice that existed will be familiar to anyone who can remember trying to pick up a girlfriend from her home and take her out as a pillion passenger.

The Japanese mounted massive advertising campaigns to destroy stereotypes. 'You meet the nicest people on a Honda' probably sums up what they were trying to achieve. The 'nicest people' campaign was introduced in America in 1962 and by the 1970s the message had reverberated around the world. As far as the Japanese were concerned, the motorcycle was to become a fashion accessory, a symbol of potency, an expensive toy, a prized possession, an inexpensive and convenient form of transport, but never again a symbol of outlaw values and bike gangs.

The 1970s were defining years for New Zealand with perhaps the most important but least acknowledged agent of change the jumbo jet. Cheap air travel had a profound effect on such a geographically isolated nation. Suddenly we were no longer an out-of-the-way country at the bottom of the globe. We could fly to Australia in a few hours or be in London, Paris or Rome in 24 hours. This would not only relieve us of the isolation, it would change New Zealand into a multi-cultural nation. It would take New Zealand to the world and bring the world to New Zealand.

In motorcycling this meant that spares that once took months to arrive, or had to be made here, suddenly appeared almost overnight. Racers who normally had to commit themselves to a whole season of racing in Europe could, by the mid-1970s, jet off to America, Japan or Europe for one-off events. When colour television arrived in New Zealand together with a second channel in 1975, live coverage of sports events became a reality. For the first time to any extent the general public was introduced to motorcycle racing.

Right above

Full-face helmets became universally acceptable in the 1970s, the American company Bell being one of the first to produce them. Locally made brands were also available and all helmets were subject to a strict safety examination and certification.

Right below

Bob Haldane was one of the road racers who thrived in the 1970s. Several generations have bought or sold bikes through Haldane's motorcycle showroom, the dealership one of the few which has lasted the distance, with Ducati now added to the long-standing Yamaha franchise. This advertisement is from the mid-1970s.

The appearance in New Zealand of 'ape hanger' handlebars coincided with the movie Easy Rider. *Nobody has ever come close to explaining why such bars, having little or nothing to do with comfort, aerodynamics, safety or good looks, should be attached to a motorcycle.*

There may be little or no direct connection between the motorcycle and the dramatic social and cultural changes that occurred during the early 1970s, except perhaps that both society and the motorcycle were in the midst of a revolution. The motorcycle did, however, play its part in popular culture. Most postwar Hollywood movies involving motorcycles perpetrated the outlaw biker theme. *The Wild One, Wild Angels, Motor Psycho* . . . the titles say it all. The 1970s opened with the highly influential *Easy Rider* which, although different, still portrayed the biker as an outcast, someone not to be trusted, someone to be taunted in restaurants and refused a room by a motel proprietor.

What seemed like a bright light on a very dark night occurred with the 1971 documentary *On Any Sunday*, dealing with the real-life world of motorcycle racing. For once a motorcyclist could go to the movies without cringing with embarrassment. That Steve McQueen played a part in the film gave it huge box-office appeal. McQueen, of course, had credibility with the motorcycle community as well as cinemagoers for the riding sequence in the movie *The Great Escape*. The truth is that McQueen didn't do the stunt riding in that movie. It was done by Tim Gibbes, an accomplished international trials rider who now lives in Palmerston North and is instrumental in promoting road racing in New Zealand. *On Any Sunday* meant that at last cinema audiences could see real people riding motorcycles, instead of drug-crazed psychopaths or sadistic killers.

Popular music of the 1970s wasn't much better than the general run of films. It had progressed little since 'Black Denim Trousers' ('He wore a black leather jacket with an eagle on the back') and 'Leader of the Pack' from the 1950s. Steppenwolf's 'Born to be Wild' from *Easy Rider* is probably the best known motorcycle song of the decade. It's harmless enough, except that it has been thrashed to death by television news producers who completely miss the point of the song.

Right above

Laurie Summers, one of a group of motorcycle dealers in Auckland's Mount Eden Road area during the 1970s, announces the arrival of the range of Kawasaki triples.

Right below

John Woodley adorns the programme cover for the short-lived Ceramco Grand Prix. Run through the streets of New Lynn in suburban Auckland, the first event in 1977 attracted international riders such as Australian Gregg Hansford and was a huge success, but there were problems with no effective way to get people to pay to watch. The second event in 1978 failed to generate the same interest and it was never run again.

Bill Russel's was one of a cluster of motorcycle dealers at the top end of Mt Eden Road in Auckland in the 1970s. Bill was a veteran of the Isle of Man and very popular among riders at the time. Here the author has just traded a Norton Commando for a CB500 Honda. European bike enthusiasts were horrified, but it was time to get into the age of the electric starter.

Celebrity endorsement is usually confined to racers, but in what seems a step further on than Honda's 'You Meet the Nicest People' campaign, Yamaha persuaded Brigette Bardot to decorate one of their products.

If you can handle power,
test-ride a Trident.

New Trident T160

Nearing the end, Triumph's revamped Trident Triple. Strangely, the designers looked back and created a bike that looks more like a Bonneville than a Trident. It was a fine looking motorcycle but failed to prevent the factory's brief slide into obscurity. Industrialist John Bloor eventually bought the name and recreated the family of successful Triumphs made today.

If imitation is the sincerest form of flattery then Triumph must take a bow. The 1999 Kawasaki W650 with the classic air-cooled parallel twin motor was about as close to a 1960s Bonneville or Daytona as could be. But in looks only. Beneath the cool, classic good looks was a thoroughly modern motorcycle made for the late 1990s and the new millennium.

Some European machines fared better than British during the Japanese revolution. Ducati started the 1970s with Paul Smart winning the prestigious Imola 200 race against the might of Japanese opposition. Towards the end of the decade in 1978 Mike Hailwood won an Isle of Man TT beating Japanese factory teams. Pictured is a 1973 750SS. This gorgeous V-twin became Ducati's signature.

They rode them to work, toured the country and raced them. The Yamaha RD250, 350 and 400s dominated the middle-weight market in the 1970s. They were great-looking bikes. They were fast, handled well, and were easy to maintain. The RDs were road-going versions of the all conquering Yamaha TZ racing two-stroke twins.

Kawasaki's potent 750 triple hit the market like a thunderbolt. Offering the sort of power normally available only on race bikes, the 500cc and 750cc two-strokes were, of course, subsequently raced with considerable success.

Kawasaki responded to Honda's six-cylinder CBX with the brutal Z1 300, also a six-cylinder machine, but it never really eclipsed the Honda in the market place.

ON THE TRACK

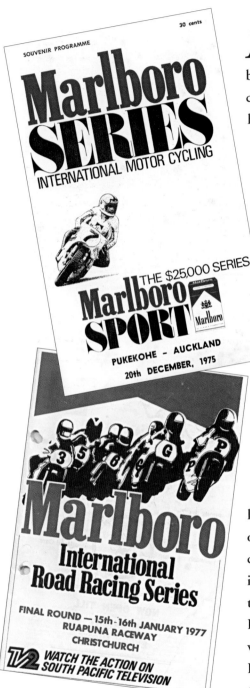

Marlboro Series programmes.

AROUND 1969, what were called 'over the counter' 250cc and 350cc Yamahas began to appear in New Zealand. These production-racing bikes, modelled on the successful World Championship winning machines, could be ordered and bought, ready to race, from a local motorcycle dealer, hence the tag. This introduced a whole generation to motorcycle racing and led into the most successful road race series ever seen in New Zealand, the Marlboro Series. Running from 1973/74 to 1977/78, it brought to New Zealand for the first time top riders from all over the world.

Not one European motorcycle made the first three in the entire period. The leading bikes were all Yamaha, Suzuki and Kawasaki, and all were two-strokes. Missing were Honda who, when they had pulled out of World Championship racing in the late 1960s, hadn't followed the example of the other three factories and made available to the public replicas of their race bikes. The exotic multi-cylinder four-strokes that they built for their works riders would, in all probability, have been far too expensive to duplicate.

The 1970s had begun with a massive injection of new machinery and competitive riders into road racing. Black leathers gave way to coloured leathers, sponsors' names began to appear on the fairings of race bikes and clothing and full-face helmets became obligatory for competition as well as common on the road.

One of the first heroes of the new decade was Geoff Perry, son of the legendary New Zealand rider of the 1950s, Len Perry. Many believed it was only a matter of time before Geoff became a World Champion. In 1971 he came second to multiple world champion Giacomo Agostini in Australia and in 1972, aged just 22, he won the Singapore Grand Prix (for the second time), the Malaysian Grand Prix and completed the Asian treble by winning in Penang. He was almost unbeatable on New Zealand circuits. Tragically, Geoff was killed in 1973 when flying to America to ride factory prepared Suzukis, his PanAm jet plunging into the sea near Tahiti. There was a great sense of loss in the motorcycle community; a feeling that we had been robbed. A naturally talented rider and a great ambassador for the sport, Geoff represented all the excitement and energy of the new Golden Age. Every year the Auckland Motorcycle Club round of the New Zealand Road Race Championships pays homage with a Geoff Perry Memorial Race.

New Zealanders began to make their mark in the blue ribbon class of the World Championships. The talented Ginger Molloy and Keith Turner came second in the 500cc class to Giacomo Agostini in 1970 and '71 respectively and the courageous Kim Newcombe came second in the same class behind Phil Read in 1973. Newcombe built and developed the German Konig machine that he rode, fighting thrilling battles with factory supported bikes on what was virtually a home-made machine. On the verge of international stardom when he was killed in a freak accident at a non-championship event in England, his engineering brilliance and ingenuity have never been fully acknowledged.

Nothing like the Marlboro Series had been seen in New Zealand before, and nothing like it has been seen since. For this reason the series has earned a special place in the history of the sport in this country. Until the Marlboro Series the best local race fans could hope for was the annual return to New Zealand of a rider who had been successful overseas. This usually meant an exhibition event with a horde of home-based riders trying to catch someone on unequal machinery.

The Marlboro Series changed all that. At last international road racing wasn't something that happened only in other countries. New Zealand saw for the first time starting grids packed with international riders. Young American rider Pat Hennen won the series three times and went on to twice claim third place in the 500cc World Championship. He was tipped to become World Champion when he was injured so badly in the Isle of Man in 1978 that he would never race again.

Italian Marco Luccinelli, who rode in the final round of the Marlboro Series, did go on to become the 500cc World Champion in 1981. Another American, Randy Mamola, rode in the Marlboro series as a teenager. After finishing in the top three of the 500cc World Championship six times, he was said to be the most talented rider never to win the World Championship.

Ginger Molloy was one of three New Zealand riders to come second in the 500cc World Championship in the early 1970s. Like Hugh Anderson, he took to racing classic bikes seriously and is still hard to beat on his Bultaco.

Trevor Discombe on a Yamaha TZ350. These two-stroke twins could hold their own with most of the bigger machines and the fact that these dedicated race bikes could be ordered from a local Yamaha dealer was a contributing factor in the road-racing boom of the 1970s. The massive drum brake would soon be replaced by discs.

TREVOR DISCOMBE

Few riders commanded as much respect as Trevor Discombe. Born in 1943, he came to prominence in the mid-1960s and was a major force in New Zealand road racing until the late '70s. He won countless New Zealand TTs and other titles, and made the transition from British to Japanese machinery. Sadly, most New Zealanders never had the chance to see some of the best racing Discombe was involved in. It took place in South-East Asia where the Japanese factories poured huge amounts of money into racing at a time when millions of Asians were switching from bicycles to motorcycles and the

big four manufacturers saw racing as a means of getting their brand name in front of the public. Discombe won Grand Prix in Malaysia, Singapore and Indonesia. His battles on the Asian circuits with Geoff Perry were sensational and well remembered by all who saw them.

In the inaugural Marlboro Series, in 1973/74, he was a close second on a TZ350 Yamaha behind Dale Wylie on a 500 Suzuki and ahead of John Boote who was riding a Yamaha TZ700. Like so many successful racers, Trevor made his future in the motorcycle industry and now runs a Honda dealership in Taumarunui.

The great American rider Cal Rayborn, who at the time was holder of the world land-speed record, was killed at Pukekohe during the second round of the Marlboro Series in 1973. Rayborn was in New Zealand to race a car but had agreed to ride in one round of the series. There was much speculation about the cause of the tragedy. An inquest established that the 500cc two-stroke, air-cooled Suzuki had seized, with one theory speculating that the motor seized because it was running on methanol. Rayborn had apparently not ridden that type of machine before. Most of his career had been spent racing big four-strokes for the Harley-Davidson factory for whom he twice won the Daytona 200.

Hideo Kanaya from Japan came for the final Marlboro Series as did British Isle of Man TT winner Chas Mortimer. From Australia came a collection of talented international riders that included Warren Willing, Gregg Hansford, Jeff and Murray Sayle, Vaughan Coburn, Graeme MacGregor, Kenny Blake and Ron Boulden. The New Zealand contingent was just as distinguished with Dennis Ireland, Graeme Crosby, Stu Avant, Trevor Discombe, John Woodley, Bob Haldane, John and Gary Boote, Dale Wylie, Rodger Freeth, Paul McLachlan, Paul Goodyer and Mike Vinsen. A comparable field in New Zealand today is difficult to imagine.

The first Marlboro Series in 1973/74 began in Wanganui then moved to Pukekohe, Gracefield and Ruapuna. The second in 1974/75 dropped Pukekohe and included Bay Park and Timaru. Then a pattern emerged and the last three were held at Pukekohe, Wanganui, Gracefield, Timaru and Ruapuna.

All the circuits were short, ranging from Pukekohe's 2.81km to Ruapuna's 1.56km. Although many of the bikes used in the Marlboro series had been developed for the longer Grand Prix or Formula 750 circuits, they proved to be just as effective on the tight New Zealand circuits. Much of the racing in the Marlboro Series was shoulder to shoulder and anyone who saw Pat Hennen, Gregg Hansford and Murray Sayle dicing through the streets of Wanganui in 1975/76 will never forget it. Afterwards Hennen said, 'I've worked harder for this title than I've ever worked before. It's been a month of absolute hell.'

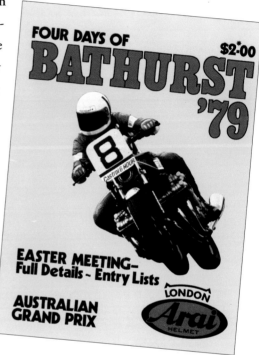

Until the coming of international Grand Prix and World Superbikes, Bathurst was the most prestigious motorcycle race venue in Australia, the mountain circuit providing the home for the Australian Grand Prix and attracting huge crowds every Easter. New Zealanders Ginger Molloy, John Woodley and Stu Avant secured victory at Bathurst between 1972 and '79, Graeme Crosby took out a second place in 1979 and Rodger Freeth won in 1985.

GEOFF PERRY

Geoff Perry was 23 years old when he died in an air-crash, cutting short a career that many believe could have given him a world championship. His success in Asia, Australia and New Zealand set the scene for his entry into the lucrative American road race scene of the early 1970s. As was the case with Trevor Discombe, most New Zealanders never had the chance to see Perry's brilliant performances in Malaysia and Singapore. It seems pointless to speculate about what he would have achieved had he survived, but those who rode with him are unanimous in their praise. Four-time world champion Hugh Anderson said that there was something in Geoff Perry's eyes, a certain look, hard to describe, but something he had seen in the eyes of other great riders.

Geoff Perry will remain one of the most treasured, and unfulfilled, figures in New Zealand motorcycle racing.

For five short years the Australians looked to New Zealand for the top road racing fixtures in the southern hemisphere and young riders all over the world were beginning to appreciate that if they did well in the Marlboro Series it would open doors in Europe and Japan. The Japanese factories were sending bikes to New Zealand that would be tested in the Marlboro Series and then raced in Europe during the northern hemisphere summer. Suddenly it all stopped. The question will always remain: If the Marlboro Series was so good, why did it stop?

The end of the series in 1978 brought the following barb from motorcycle journalist Don Cox: 'The loss of the Marlboro Series is indeed a sad one, and one that will put the cause back more years than most of us would like to consider.' He blamed, among other things, 'amateur organizers biting off more than they could chew'. Others blame the withdrawal of sponsorship. Maybe it was simply the end of an era; maybe it was just part of the 1970s. The total prize money for the Marlboro Series in 1976 was $30,000. The money demanded today by riders of the calibre of Hennen, Luccinelli and Mamola would bankrupt promoters.

Ten years later, in 1988, New Zealand staged a round of the inaugural Superbike World Championship at Manfeild. International road racing was back on the agenda, but not for long. There would only be three more, in 1989, 1990 and 1992.

Stu Avant lifts the front wheel of his Yamaha as he challenges Kenny Fletcher just before the pedestrian crossing on the streets of Wanganui during the Marlboro Series. Protection for spectators has become more stringent since this shot was taken.

Kim Newcombe's brilliance as an engineer and rider was never fully realised. On a bike he had virtually built himself he came second in the 500cc World Championship of 1973 behind Phil Read and ahead of Giacomo Agostini, both riding works MV Agustas.

Racing will always improve the breed. It is the most competitive form of motorcycle activity and everyone in the end benefits from the research and development that goes into racing. Following the halcyon days of the Marlboro Series there seems little to cheer about in New Zealand, but there will be other ways in which the sport will flourish. There is certainly no shortage of class riders. In recent years John Hepburn, Tony Rees, Jason McKewen, Andrew Stroud and Dean Fulton have brought some exciting racing to home circuits, and Aaron Slight and Simon Crafar have raised the flag internationally. Road racing in New Zealand is going through that agonising transformation between amateur and professional organisation of the sport. Resistance from the establishment who want things done the way they have been for the last 60 years will frustrate the new breed for a while, but eventually we will end up with a with a sport which has the potential to lift major sponsorship from less exciting forms of entertainment.

Dennis Ireland and Peter Pawson, two of the quicker Kiwis in the late 1970s. Here they display the uncanny ability to have broken the same wrist at the same time. Perhaps they thought the vintage Harley-Davidson they are riding would be a safe bet until they could get back on racing machinery.

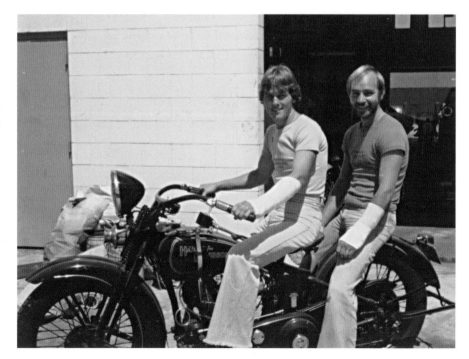

The starting grid for the Dunedin Festival Road Races of 1979. The racing that followed was a matter of cut-and-thrust between the kerbs and lampposts of the city streets. The author, in red leathers, is on a Manx Norton with an ES2 motor.

The Castrol lady appears to be preventing a happy Dave Hiscock from being lubricated with the bubbly stuff as he is about to talk to the crowd after winning the 1980 Adelaide Three-Hour race. One of many Kiwis successful across the Tasman during this period, Dave had a younger brother, Neville who also raced with success in Australia, but he was tragically killed in 1983 during a race in South Africa.

Future and past world champions meet in the Pukekohe paddock as Marco Lucchinelli (left) talks to Mike Hailwood during the final Marlboro Series, in 1977/78. Had he not broken his collarbone halfway through the series, Lucchinelli would have been more competitive in New Zealand . . . but a bigger prize would come the Italian's way in 1981 in the form of the 500cc World Championship.

The ultra-slick Pat Hennen rips through the curves at Levels with Gregg Hansford all but leaning on him. Both riders were stars of the Marlboro Series and subsequently covered themselves with glory in Europe. With success in Finland in 1976, Hennen became the first American to win a World Championship Grand Prix while Hansford, the only rider to seriously challenge Hennen in New Zealand in the 1975/76 series, won ten Grand Prix.

Poster for the final Marlboro Series. The picture was taken during the 1976/77 series in Wanganui. The riders are Ken Fletcher, Yamaha 700 (4); Mike Vinsen, Yamaha 350 (49); Pat Hennen, Suzuki 500 (P); Vaughan Coburn, Yamaha 350 (C3); Ian Scattergood, Yamaha 350 (C6); Jeff Sayle, Suzuki 500 (J); Stu Avant, Yamaha 750 (1); John Marsh, Yamaha 350 (68). The imposing shape of Graeme Crosby on the Yoshimura Kawasaki can be seen shadowing Hennen.

Tension mounts and adrenaline pumps as Gregg Hansford, Pat Hennen, Sadao Asami and Stu Avant between them unleash more than 500 horsepower at the beginning of one of the Marlboro rounds in 1977.

Four of the most significant riders of the early 1970s. From left to right: Keith Turner, Ginger Molloy, Trevor Discombe and Geoff Perry. They all raced with distinction in New Zealand, Turner and Molloy going on to make their names in Europe and Discombe and Perry in Asia.

A well tucked in Pat Hennen guns his Suzuki RG500-4 along the short straight at Levels, in Timaru. Although these machines were developed for much longer European Grand Prix circuits, they were very effective on the short and twisty New Zealand track and street circuits. The square four configured 500cc two-strokes won Suzuki the manufacturers' 500cc World Championship for seven consecutive years from 1976.

Is there anyone behind me? Paul McLachlan from Christchurch takes a hurried look over his shoulder as he releases the driving power of his TZ750 onto the long, fast back straight at Pukekohe in 1977. McLachlan, a first rate mechanic and engineer, was renowned for his consistency as a rider and raced with some success in America.

Warren Willing on the starting grid at Levels in Timaru. The popular Australian was second behind Pat Hennen in the 1976/77 Marlboro Series and third behind the Sayle brothers Murray and Jeff the following year. His career as a rider ended in 1979 at the North West 200 street race in Northern Ireland, a series of eighteen operations being needed to enable him to walk again following a horrific crash. Willing has never deserted the sport and has found a place in several Grand Prix management and technical teams.

A pensive Gregg Hansford studies his winner's trophy, with second placed John Woodley applauding and third man home Trevor Discombe finding other distractions.

If Australian Vaughan Coburn didn't attract a lot of attention on the track, the art work on the fairing of his Yamaha certainly did in the paddock. The work of painter Alan Puckett, the decoration made the bike one of the most talked about, looked at and photographed and proved a clever method of gaining exposure for his sponsors.

Three great competitors in Bob Haldane, John Woodley and Rodger Freeth on the podium at Hawkesbury in 1980. Woodley seems delighted with his second place, probably because his Suzuki converted to hand gear change in the middle of the race.

Simon Crafar examines the boundaries of adhesion on the 500cc Red Bull Yamaha. Ironically it was a team decision to change tyre manufacturers, and Crafar's failure to come to grips with the new brand was said to have contributed to the decline of his Grand Prix fortunes.

Phil Read, the man who led the revival in the Isle of Man in 1977, won 52 Grand Prix and seven world championships. The last two, in 1973 and '74 on an MV Agusta, were the last 500cc four-stoke victories until the class specifications changed in 2002.

John Woodley and Pat Hennen approaching the railway lines that run across the track at the Wanganui Street circuit. The regular Boxing Day fixture attracts some of the largest crowds of any motor sport event in New Zealand.

Pat Hennen (you can see his leathers) stands between the Yamahas of Stu Avant and Warren Willing in the Gracefield paddock near Wellington. Willing's bike is the TZ750 formerly ridden by Giacomo Agostini. International race paddocks enjoyed a much more relaxed atmosphere than they do today and it was easy to wander around, talk to the riders and look at the bikes.

The author waiting for clearance to ride Bob Haldane's TZ700 at Pukekohe. The power came from basically two TZ350 two-stroke twin motors. The next model became the TZ750, the machine used by Mike Hailwood to prepare for his return to the Isle of Man in 1978. Hailwood is wearing leathers and jumper and standing second from the right. This bike has been restored and runs in Post-Classic meetings in New Zealand to this day.

It was never going to happen. Talented designer and accomplished racer Dr Rodger Freeth, tragically killed in a rally car accident in the 1980s, designed this aerofoil to stabilise a race bike at speed. The authorities decided it would destabilise other riders on the track.

Stu Avant from Christchurch won the Australian 500cc Grand Prix in 1978. Here he takes a badly needed drink in the South Australian heat at Adelaide International Raceway before the start of a race.

Left

Geoff Perry aboard the 500cc twin-cylinder, two-stroke Suzuki. Developed from the road-going machine, they were the quickest 500s of their day and were eventually superseded by the RG500 square four.

Below

Geoff Perry joins a gallery of stars in America. From left, Perry, Australian Kel Carruthers, Britons Phil Read, Tony Jefferies and Peter Williams and Yvonne du Hamel from Canada. Road racing flourished in America during the 1970s with big prize money attracting riders.

Above

The streets can be an uncompromising environment. Many riders are beginning to question the safety of our street races.

Right

Robert Holden was one of the most popular New Zealand riders of the 1980s and '90s. He rode the 'Plastic fantastic' machine designed by Steve Roberts with great success at New Zealand street circuits. Holden was killed in the Isle of Man when he lost control of his Ducati during practice. He first raced on the island in 1992, winning the Supermono single-cylinder class in 1995. At the time of his death Holden was on top of the practice leader board in two classes, and had just set his fastest ever TT lap at 120.38 mph.

They don't attract the same sponsorship and support given to the solo classes, but sidecars are always popular on street circuits and do have a loyal following. They are exciting to watch close up as they twitch and flick through corners.

Former works Triumph and Ducati rider Paul Smart came to New Zealand in 1998 with a 750cc Ducati, the bike he used to win the Italian classic, the Imola 200, in 1972. In 2002 he returned to Pukekohe, bringing a works Triumph triple which he had ridden in the early 1970s. The picture shows him about to mount the Ducati.

Chas Mortimer crosses the railway lines at Wanganui before the start of a race in the final Marlboro Series. The Englishman's experience in the Isle of Man gave him the necessary skills to succeed on New Zealand street circuits.

A mixture of smoke — the result of a predominantly two-stroke field — and excitement gets the big field away in Wanganui.

It's doubtful that any of the riders from the current Grand Prix or Superbike scene would ride in street races. Not so when this shot was taken at Wanganui in 1977. There are, however, street specialists who ride in Northern Ireland, the Isle of Man and certain parts of Europe who still visit New Zealand.

Stu Avant heads for pit-lane after a street race at Gracefield near Wellington at the final Marlboro Series. Gracefield was the least interesting of street circuits and at a little over two kilometres very short.

SPEEDWAY

Speedway was arguably not only the first form of off-road racing in New Zealand, but also the first of any form of motorcycle racing. That is, if we accept that racing on an oval track covered in grass or dirt, and using the foot to slide around corners, is close enough to be called speedway.

There are two theories about the origins of speedway. It either began as dirt-track racing in America, when motorcyclists took over horse-trotting tracks, or at the New South Wales Agricultural Show. In New Zealand, motorcycle racing on horse-racing tracks was popular before the First World War. The most important fact, however, is that speedway arrived in Britain in 1927 and within a year a race meeting attracted 20,000 spectators. The first floodlit meeting took place in 1928 and in 1936 the first World Championship, under the auspices of the FIM, was held at Wembley Stadium in London. Riders came from Australia, Sweden, New Zealand, Germany, Canada, France, America, Denmark, Britain, Spain and South Africa. Speedway had arrived as a major sport and by the 1970s speedway was Britain's second-largest spectator sport, behind soccer.

Although speedway has never been embraced by mainstream motorcycle racing, it has always been a recognised branch of motorcycle sport. Two aspects separate modern speedway from other forms of motorcycle sport – manufacturers have never been involved in speedway on a competitive basis and speedway bikes are so specialised that they have no application away from a purpose-built race track.

In nearly 70 years there have been only minimal design changes to speedway bikes and during that time three manufacturers, one after another, have dominated the sport – JAP engines ruled for the first 30 years, followed by JAWA and, from 1973, Westlake. All were 500cc four-strokes with a single cylinder, the JAP and JAWA engines with two valves, the Westlake four, and all run on methanol. The most purposeful and minimalist motorcycles ever conceived, they have only one gear, virtually no suspension and as they have no brakes they must be controlled with the clutch and throttle.

BARRY BRIGGS

Barry Briggs was four times world speedway champion and the second of three riders from Christchurch to win individual World Speedway Championships. Although his ambition to equal the record five world championships won by Swede Ove Funden came up just short, Ivan Mauger later made sure the record would come to New Zealand by winning six titles.

Briggs appeared in no fewer than eighteen world championship finals, his distinguished career beginning when he followed his good friend and idol Ronnie Moore to England. Apart from his many British speedway league achievements, he rode in every speedway country in the world, won four individual world titles and also has a world team title to his credit.

IVAN MAUGER

Few would argue that Ivan Mauger was the greatest of all speedway riders. The ultimate professional both and off the track, his preparation and attention to detail meant that he won most of his races from the starting gate.

He won six individual world championships and was awarded an MBE in 1976. In 2000 the influential Speedway Star and Vintage Speedway magazines asked their readers to vote for the best 100 riders of all time. Mauger won with ease ahead of Denmark's Hans Nielson and Sweden's Ove Funden. In 1987 the governing body of international motorcycle sport, the FIM, awarded him the Gold Medal. This places Mauger alongside the likes of Giacomo Agostini and Wayne Rainey, and the only New Zealander apart from John Britten to win the award.

One speedway rider rose like a colossus above every other competitor in the 1970s. Ivan Mauger started his career in Christchurch in 1956 and by 1979 had won six individual World Championships, three in successive years, 1968, '69 and '70, the others coming in 1972, '77 and '79. He was awarded an MBE in 1976. Mauger followed two other New Zealanders to World Speedway Championship honours. Barry Briggs, also from Christchurch, won four individual World Championships in 1957, '58, '64 and '66. He was also awarded an MBE, in 1973.

The third rider of the extraordinarily talented trio was Ronnie Moore, who was born in Tasmania but moved to New Zealand when he was very young. He first came to prominence as a rider when he won the South Island Speedway Championship at the age of sixteen. Soon after he went to Europe, and won two World Championships, in 1954 and '59. That's a total of twelve World Championships between three riders in 25 years – surely a feat unequalled in any branch of New Zealand sport. It is interesting that when Great Britain won speedway's Team World Championship for the first time, in 1968, Barry Briggs was team captain. By 1979 New Zealand could stand on its own feet, and took out the Team World Championship for New Zealand.

Unlike Europe, where speedway means bikes, in New Zealand, more often than not, it means cars. Our successful speedway riders enjoyed a level of popularity and recognition in Europe they could only dream of in their own country, and most of the bench at an NPC rugby game would be better known in New Zealand than our world-class riders.

It is fair to say that since the 1970s speedway has lost some of its appeal, although it's doing well in northern Europe, with riders coming from Australia and America to compete. Speedway now faces competition from the new forms of motorcycle sport like supercross, which can also be staged in a stadium under lights. Our Maugers and Moores of the new millennium may be called Coppins and King.

Chapter 7

BACK TO THE FUTURE

IT seemed that in the 1970s the four major factories developed their own trade-mark models – Kawasaki the fearsome two-stroke triples and Z1; Suzuki the rotary and water-cooled triple; Honda the Gold Wing and CB750; Yamaha the brilliant small-bore two-stroke twins. All these models were undeniably associated with the factory which made them and their specifications were as different as their descriptions suggest.

What appeared to happen after the experiments of the 1970s was a settling-down period followed by each factory turning out an almost identical range of bikes . . . only the names on the tank varied. Look at the way all four factories followed one another by producing a turbo-charged model in the early 1980s. Maybe if one or two had developed the turbo as a brand mark it may have worked – four versions of everything seems just too much. Look how at the end of the 1990s every Japanese factory had a competitive 600cc, 750cc and 1000cc four-cylinder four-stroke bike.

Once on the treadmill the factories can't get off. The only way to get a jump on the opposition is to bring out a new model every year, with sometimes as little change as a new paint job and two extra horsepower. This, of course, becomes unpopular with the buying public who see the value of their bike diminishing almost by the day. Only the later return of the Europeans and the rebirth of Harley-Davidson would eventually offer the buying public an alternative.

From another perspective, the Japanese used racing in the 1960s to experiment and develop the technology that would power the bikes they would sell to the public in the 1970s – Suzuki perfected the small two-stroke machines ridden by Hugh Anderson; Yamaha the four-cylinder 125cc and 250cc water-cooled two-strokes ridden by Bill Ivey and Phil Read; Honda an array of four-, five- and six-cylinder bikes ridden by Jim Redman and Mike Hailwood. In the same period Italy's MV Agusta produced two-, three-, four-, five- and six-cylinder racers and Moto Guzzi built and raced a 500cc V8, but unlike the Japanese little if any of this technology reached road bikes that people could buy.

Most of the Japanese factories deserted the racetrack at the end of the 1960s, their R&D for the moment done. They did return to racing during the 1970s, but by the beginning of the 1980s, as so often happens with technology, the four factories had established the most economical and effective ways to mass produce motorcycles and, surprise surprise, they had all come up with similar solutions.

The 1980s witnessed the Japanese factories fighting to keep the momentum of the 1970s going. As well as the ploy of churning out new models at an alarming rate, there was a push into the new areas of off-road biking. By the end of the decade motorcycling was heading for the leisure markets and as cars became cheaper the commuter market for motorcycles began to shrink, eventually killed off in New Zealand by the mass importing of cheap Japanese used cars.

Some mourned the demise of the small, cheap bikes but the people riding them were never motorcyclists in the true sense of the word. Bikes were now being bought to ride for fun and pleasure as well as transport. Those who could afford big bikes, often more expensive than cars, usually had a car for mundane chores and a bike for the weekends – something like owning a boat.

It was this change of direction that signalled the return of the Europeans. They knew how to make desirable, low-volume machines that held their value in the market place. They also understood a phenomenon particularly relevant to motorcyclists – identification with a marque and pride of ownership.

One of the most effective transformations in motorcycle history was the revival of Harley-Davidson. From a machine with a reputation for unreliability and a strong association with outlaw bike gangs, Harley became the darling of movie stars, sports heroes and intrepid executives. Harley boutiques sprang up all over the world. We now have Harley-Davidson branded products from fashionable clothing to after-shave. By the late 1990s Harley-Davidson was the third best selling bike in New Zealand behind Honda and Suzuki.

No it isn't an early Bonneville. It is a thoroughly modern 21st-century Triumph Bonneville, built at the Hinckley factory in the hope that the appearance and the charisma attached to the name would still attract customers. It certainly did and the bike sold well everywhere.

JOHN BRITTEN

A friend once told me that a young John Britten used to come to his garage in Christchurch to look at and ask questions about his Vincent. Young John seemed fascinated by the big British V-twins, as have motorcycle enthusiasts since production ceased in 1955. A devotion to the V-twin configuration is familiar to motorcyclists. From the Bologna factory of Ducati, to Harley-Davidson's Milwaukee headquarters, the V-twin has an army of devotees. Much of John's early work was with Ducati engines.

John Britten's achievements are phenomenal. It would be easy to say that he had more money and support than many of our earlier innovators, but compared with the multi-national companies his machines would compete with, his resources were modest. Britten produced ten models. A pre-cursor in 1988 had conventional front forks and was powered by the first Britten engines to be cast. Bike number one had interchangeable 1000cc and 1100cc engines. The bike was hand-crafted by John and his team and the moulds for the bodywork and other parts evolved and were used in all subsequent models. Number two is in Te Papa in Wellington. This bike broke four national land speed records and was the first locally built bike to win the New Zealand Grand Prix. Number three competed at the Isle of Man and was the first Britten to be sold. Number four won at Daytona. Number five competed at the Isle of Man, as did number six. Number seven resides in an

Andrew Stroud displays one of only ten Brittens ever made.

American museum and number eight is a Daytona winner. Number nine was raced in Japan, the United States and Europe, and ten, although tested by Jason McEwen at Ruapuna, is the only Britten never raced. It was also the last of the hand-built Brittens.

Perhaps the saddest aspect of Britten motorcycles is that they could never race in Grand Prix or World Superbikes. Rule changes in Moto GP in 2002 may have made it possible, but it's too late. The natural hunting ground for the Britten would have been the Superbikes, but Britten could never build enough bikes to satisfy the homologation requirements.

This doesn't distract from John Britten's massive contribution to engineering and motorcycling. That he could build a motorcycle in this country that would be revered all over the world is something that should never be forgotten.

Aaron Slight (3) being chased by Britain's Carl Fogarty during the 1996 Superbike World Championship. Slight finished the season second with Fogarty fourth.

AARON SLIGHT

Aaron Slight's Superbike career was remarkable. His record between 1993 and '98 stands at two second and four third places in the world championship – six years in the top three. In 1999 he slipped to fourth. To call him the unluckiest rider in the short history of World Superbike racing would not be a exaggeration. Slight was hampered by a succession of crashes, most of which were sheer bad luck. His superb standard of physical fitness helped him through the resulting injuries. The final injustice was a brain tumour – corrected by surgery – which plagued him through his final two seasons.

As always there are many theories why Aaron Slight didn't win a world championship. Should he, for example, have left Honda in the mid-1990s and found himself a Ducati? Whatever should have happened, he is still our most successful rider of the 1990s. On top of his impressive World Superbike record, he won the most prestigious race in Japan, the Suzuka Eight-Hour, for three consecutive years, in 1993, '94 and '95, with three different co-riders. He was also Australian Superbike Champion in 1991.

Bill Buckley built New Zealand's first Grand Prix racer at his Auckland factory in the late 1990s. It was tough going against the major manufacturers and the works machinery but he earned the respect of race fans everywhere.

Things were stirring in Europe too. The much-loved Triumph was reborn in Britain, successfully going in to bat against a Rising Sun that had all but destroyed it in the 1970s. BMW found new fields. Apart from their popular road bikes they moved into adventure and off-road machines, enjoying great success in the Paris to Dakar rally. The most spectacular European success during the 1990s was Ducati, the relatively small Italian factory taking on the big Japanese brands and dominating world Superbike racing for most of the decade. Ducati set an example for other Italian marques and Aprilia, MV Agusta and Benelli produced very desirable bikes going into the 21st century.

Although the reborn British and Europeans are back on track they are not producing the numbers of the big Japanese companies. But their success is good for the motorcycling public as it means greater choice, more ideas and ultimately better products.

Could there be another Golden Age on the horizon? It is difficult to imagine how the Japanese phenomenon could happen again on such a scale and it's fair to say that both the automobile and the motorcycle will have to reinvent themselves in the near future.

The growth areas for the motorcycle are likely to be not in transport but in leisure. The off-road riding community is undoubtedly the fastest growing sector in New Zealand. Vast numbers of people, from small children to weathered veterans, ride along the forests tracks and over the sand dunes every weekend. Others explore the thousands of kilometres of unsealed roads that provide an outlet for adventure riding.

Sport is another growth area. The sixteen Grand Prix rounds in 2001 were watched by 1,500,000 spectators, an increase of 10 per cent over the previous year. That these races and the Superbike World Championship are beamed into our living rooms from Europe and elsewhere must increase awareness of the sport. In New Zealand 5000 people bought racing licences for the 2001/02 season. Motocross and supercross are gaining fresh support all the time, again helped by a regular diet of international events on television.

Although there are fewer motorcycles on our roads than in the halcyon days of the 1970s, there is more choice. There are sports bikes and touring bikes,

KEN McINTOSH

Along with Burt Munro, John Britten, Steve Roberts and Bill Buckley, Ken McIntosh has established himself as a New Zealand motorcycle innovator. Ken McIntosh's work on Manx Nortons has alone given him a worldwide reputation, but he also achieved some remarkable success with his McIntosh Suzukis, which in their day were exceptionally competitive bikes.

The McIntosh workshop in Auckland can make about 50 per cent of the necessary parts to build a 1962 Manx Norton. In fact, the whole chassis is made in the workshop. The quality of Ken's workmanship is respected everywhere classic racing is part of the calendar, and he must take much of the credit for the huge increase in the popularity of the class in New Zealand.

CRAFAR "HARKA"

An artist's impression of Simon Crafar following his victory in the 1998 British Grand Prix.

sports tourers and cruisers, naked bikes and faired bikes . . . in fact bikes for all occasions. The machines are more exotic, their uses and style more clearly defined. Many of the changes and much of the development is, of course, a legacy of the 1970s.

An interesting development at the end of the 1990s saw the Italian Cagiva company put Suzuki engines into their Raptor 650cc and 1000cc models. Shared componentry, including agreements between Japanese factories, is well and truly on the agenda. The old British bikes used to have Lucas electrics and Smiths instruments. The modern Triumph factory sources components from wherever they find what they want.

Specialist companies making specialised equipment makes perfect sense, but what looks to be happening is not quite like that. It could come to one company making wheels and brakes, another the chassis, another the engine and the fourth electrics and ignition.

Have you ever gone to a car park and found that all the cars look the same? Have you ever thought that the car manufacturers must all be using the same wind tunnel? Don't panic. In the motorcycle world you can still tell a Harley from a Ducati, a Suzuki from a BMW. But certain sectors could be under threat. Line up four current Japanese sportsbikes and mentally take off the decals and the distinctive paint job. Now say if you can tell the difference from 30 metres. The innovative nation that gave us the motorcycle revolution of the 1970s, with the distinctive models from the big four factories, is in danger of producing a bike called a Sukahonya. Let's hope nobody buys it.

Above

Aaron Slight came tantalisingly close to being the first New Zealander since Graeme Crosby to win a World Championship, but it just wouldn't happen.

Left

A beautifully restored BSA Rocket at Pukekohe. The triple-cylinder 750cc engines were built by the BSA/Triumph collaboration during the late 1960s and '70s, the Triumph version being the Trident. They were raced with considerable success and almost won Daytona.

The tyre-shredding horsepower at the back wheel of the 1000cc V-twin Britten is demonstrated by Andrew Stroud at Pukekohe. The still-radical design draws crowds whenever it appears at race meetings around the country. Features such as the rear-mounted radiator have been copied on more recent designs such as the Italian Benelli Tornado.

Andrew Stroud retains strong links with the Britten family. He is seen here with John Britten's daughter while waiting for the start of the Superbike race in the New Zealand Road Race Championships at Levels, Timaru, in 1998.

Having narrowly avoided bankruptcy, Harley-Davidson staged a revival that saw the marque command the greatest brand loyalty of almost any motorcycle. Above is the trusty Sportster Evolution engine, a stalwart in the Harley range for many years.

The first radical departure from the simple traditional air-cooled Harley twin (left). Although still a V-twin, the V-Rod is powered by a water-cooled 1000cc motor with eight valves and fuel injection. The V-Rod sparked an interest in long, low and lean hot rod-like bikes, adding another spectrum to the list of different styles of bike on the market.

One of the most distinguished motorcycle journalists in the world, Englishman Alan Cathcart's road and track tests cover a vast selection of vintage, classic and modern machinery. Here he rides a McIntosh Norton at the Pukekohe Classic meeting in 1998. Unfortunately, a crash at this meeting sent him home with a broken leg.

Simon Crafar's YZR500cc works Yamaha. In 1998 the four-cylinder two-stroke carried Crafar to victory ahead of Mick Doohan in the British Grand Prix and second to the multiple world champion at the Australian Grand Prix.

Chris Haldane, son of 1970s icon Bob, lifts the front wheel of his Ducati in Wanganui. Ducati was the first European brand to regain some ground from the Japanese on the race track.

Mark Willis aboard the BSL. The bike, built in Auckland, is a three-cylinder two-stroke 500cc Grand Prix racer and made a few appearances at selected Grand Prix. Many things conspired to prevent the BSL from succeeding, among them the might and development potential of the Japanese factories and the coming of 1000cc four-strokes in Grand Prix racing which saw a declining interest in two-strokes.

The longing for the looks of another era. This Kawasaki Drifter is a 2000 model but it looks for all the world like a 1948 Indian. But there the comparison ends. This is a 1500cc twin cylinder motor, with single overhead cam and eight valves. It is liquid cooled, fuel injected and has sophisticated suspension.

The TZ Yamaha, one of the 'over the counter' Yamaha racers that did so much to inject life into road racing in the 1970s. The two-stroke 250cc and 350cc twins offered aspiring racers a weapon that would put them in among the top riders, if they had the ability. The later models were water-cooled. Yamaha eventually bolted two 350 motors together to produce the formidable TZ700 two-stroke four. Pictured here is a YZR350.

It was unthinkable in the 1970s, an Italian bike with a Japanese engine. The Italian Cagiva Raptors come with a 650cc or 1000cc V-twin Suzuki motor, with the result a very well balanced machine with both style and reliability.

Having led the way for 30 years, the Japanese looked again to Europe. It was the success of the Ducati 90° V-twins in Superbike racing that prompted Honda to produce their own V-twin. The VTR SP1 won the Superbike title in its first season. This superb engine is also to be used in the reborn Italian marque Mondial, another marriage of Japanese engine and Italian chassis design. The picture is a road-going version of the VTR SP1.

A Post-Classic field lines up at Pukekohe in 2000. These bikes, predominantly from the 1970s, are beginning to attract big crowds and because there is so much Post-Classic machinery around, more and more mature riders are deciding to go racing in this class.

The great Giacomo Agostini, fifteen times world champion, came to New Zealand in 1999 with a collection of the fabulous MV Agustas he rode in the 1960s and '70s. Interest in the men and machines from that era was reinforced by the huge crowd that turned out to see him.

John Britten and Bill Buckley had the race track firmly in their sights when they built their respective machines, but Auckland motorcycle dealer and bike builder Ray Pratt had no such ambition when he build Road Rage, a big and powerful custom cruiser. In 2002 the hand-built machine entered its fifth year of production. When the author, pictured, rode the 1999 model it was producing 110hp at the rear wheel, but the latest model improves on that by more than 10hp. The 45-degree V-twin engine measured 1850cc. The chassis, tank, front and rear guards, side panels and seat were all made in New Zealand, the engine and other components come from the United States. Road Rage is custom built for each buyer, so it is unlikely there will be two exactly the same, which makes it a very exclusive Kiwi product.

BIKES OF THE CENTURY

When the year 2000 was on the horizon motorcycle magazines all over the world scrambled to elect their 'Bike of the century'. Given the global nature of motorcycling perhaps it isn't surprising that most of them came up with very similar results. The Honda CB750 won in most countries. In *New Zealand Motorcycle Trader & News* magazine readers elected the following: 1. Honda CB750; 2. Triumph Bonneville; 3. Kawasaki Z1; 4. Yamaha RD 350/400; 5. BSA Gold Star; 6. Honda C100; 7. Norton Commando; 8. Honda CBX; 9. Suzuki T20. The most noticeable absence is bikes made after 1980. Maybe this is an indication that bikes must first become classics and prove their lasting qualities before motorcyclists are prepared to give them legendary status. The bikes are featured on the following pages together with a few that were given honorary mention.

1969 HONDA CB750

From 1968/69 until 1977/78, Honda built almost a million CB750s, undoubtedly one of the most influential motorcycles of the past 50 years The bike paved the way for the in-line four cylinder engine to become the benchmark for almost every big four-stroke to leave the Japanese factories until the present day. The CB750 dealt an almost fatal blow to the British motorcycle industry and rocked the rest of the Japanese industry, who scrambled to catch up. Honda had made a sophisticated and potent motorcycle, with refinements usually found only on works racing bikes, available to the public at a price people could afford. The CB750 produced 67bhp with a top speed of 185kph.

TRIUMPH BONNEVILLE 650

The origins of the Triumph Bonneville, an icon of the golden age of British bikes, go back to 1937 when Edward Turner created his legendary 498cc ohv vertical Speed Twin, a design that formed the basis for Triumph twins until the 1970s. The name Bonneville comes from the Utah salt flats where in 1956 a streamlined T110 Triumph was clocked, unofficially, at 343kph. The Bonneville was a development of the Tiger T110. Some of the early models did little to stir the imagination, but in the early 1960s the legend began to take shape. By 1969, the year that the Bonnie received the twin leading shoe front brake, it became the first production bike to lap the Isle of Man at over 100mph and it is the Triumph Bonneville of that period which most people look upon with affection. The Bonnie, however, was made in some shape or form from 1959 to '98, so there will be many differing opinions about which one is better. The 649cc T120 produced 46bhp at 6500rpm with a top speed of 177kph.

1973 KAWASAKI 900 Z1

It took Kawasaki only three years to respond to the sensation caused by Honda's CB750. In 1972 the 900 Z1 was launched and a new legend was born. Like the Honda, the Z1 was an in-line four-cylinder, air-cooled four-stroke. The Kawasaki did have double overhead cams compared with a single on the Honda, it was 167cc bigger and there were differences with the bearings, crank, and primary drive, but what caught the imagination of the buying public was its performance. The Z1 soon became known as 'The King', the road-going superbike that set new standards for others to follow. In 1972 only works racers produced 82bhp. The Z1 could deliver that at 8500rpm on the road, in standard trim. Top speed was around 215kph. The engine provided the basis for the big bore Kawasaki range through to 1984, but purists say that the 1972 and '73 models are the quintessential Z1s.

YAMAHA RD350/400

The RD Yamahas occupy a special place in the history of New Zealand motorcycling. These efficient, simple, two-stroke twins could be ridden to work during the week and on weekends stripped of their road legal requirements and thrashed around a race-track. What is more, they could hold their own with bikes twice their size. Many of our leading racers cut their teeth on an RD250 or 350. The RDs would later have the suffix LC added when they were liquid-cooled. In 1973 Yamaha introduced reed-valve induction on the first RDs. This involved a one-way valve between the carburettor and crankcase which allowed for higher crankcase pressure without risking 'blowback' through the carburettor, an induction system which is a feature of Grand Prix bikes to this day. The TZ series of race bikes, which have dominated certain classes of racing for around 25 years, are direct relatives of the Yamaha RD250/350.

BSA GOLD STAR DBD34 500

One of the most glamorous names in motorcycle history, Gold Star comes from a lapel badge that was given to riders in the 1930s who completed a lap of the old Brooklands circuit in England at over the ton (100mph). There were 350 Gold Stars in the 1940s, one of which won the 1949 Clubman's TT on the Isle of Man, and although this was the beginning of outstanding track success, it is the 500 that brought the model universal recognition by road riders. Regarded as the definitive Gold Star, the DBD34 was an uncompromising machine considered by many to be noisy, uncomfortable and temperamental, but these very characteristics made the bike exciting and attractive to legions of boy racers who blasted along the highways from the mid-1950s to the mid-'60s. After all, that's what racing bikes were like. The Goldie, as it became known, had a two-valve, push-rod, single-cylinder 499cc engine. It produced between 38 and 42bhp at 7000rpm, with a top speed of 160kph.

HONDA C100

The little 50cc Honda, or Honda Cub, moved half the world from bicycles to motorcycles and is sometimes called the two-wheeled Model T Ford. In 1958 and '59 the Japanese home market swallowed the entire production run of 750,000. When the C100 arrived in Asia it changed completely the characteristics of city traffic. It also found acceptance in Africa and South America. Millions were sold all over the world. As a result, Soichiro Honda became the first foreigner to be awarded a place in the American Motorcycling Hall of Fame. The original C100 was built until 1967. It was followed by the C50, which is exactly the same concept with a few engineering refinements, such as an overhead camshaft engine. In total more than 15 million C100 and C50s have been sold. It is still available today and has made it into the 21st century.

NORTON COMMANDO

The Commando started life as a 750 and ended up an 850. It is the final development of a British parallel twin that began in 1948. In the late 1960s Norton was close to collapse. The new Commando engine, with its forward inclined cylinders designed by Dr Stefan Bauer, was to be the saviour of the factory. The Commando design also addressed vibration, the curse of British parallel twins. Norton devised a system involving the use of rubber shims to isolate the engine, gearbox, and the swinging arm from the rest of the motorcycle. The shims had to be kept in near-perfect condition or the handling would suffer. The Commando engine was used in the John Player Norton on which Peter Williams won the 1973 Formula 750 Isle of Man TT. At the time he was the third fastest man around the island circuit after Hailwood and Agostini. It was one of the last glimmers of hope for the British industry as the Japanese wave gained momentum. Fifty-five thousand Commandos were built. Many came to New Zealand, and a John Player Replica has been seen in this country.

HONDA CBX6 1000

Honda's six-cylinder CBX, a technological masterpiece with 24 valves, six carburettors and four hollow camshafts, was inspired by the exciting six-cylinder racing machines of the 1960s. At 105bhp, the air-cooled powerplant was the first production engine to exceed the magic 100bhp. Amazingly, the engine of the CBX weighs less than that of a CB750 and, measured over the crankcases, the slim straight six is also narrower than the CB750. The CBX never became a top seller for Honda and the model had a short life span. It did, however, quickly achieve classic status and a well kept or restored one is treated with respect to this day.

SUZUKI T20 250

In the mid-1960s, when the 250cc class was as fiercely competitive as the 600cc class of today, the T20 two-stroke twin was the bike that put Suzuki into pole position. It had six gears, was fast, light and handled well and was also simple to maintain. A few T20s were sold in 1965 but it really gained ground in 1966 when the little Suzuki became the first Oriental bike to be named motorcycle of the year by Britain's prestigious Motorcycle News. Manufactured until 1970, the T20, which produced 29bhp and weighed only 135kg, was in the vanguard of the two-stroke 250s that began to beat 500 and 750 four-strokes on the racetracks of the 1970s. It is now very popular in post-classic racing circles.

SUZUKI 1100 KATANA

By the early 1980s Suzuki had developed an extremely powerful and compact in-line four-cylinder engine. It had the magic prefix GSX. In their efforts to find a design to match the performance of the dohc 16-valve engine, the company turned to former BMW car designer Jan Fellstrom. The Suzuki Katana was the result. Characterised by its integral fuel tank and seat, half-fairing and two-tone seat, the Katana was an immediate hit with riders wanting style, reliability and high performance. Although in the early 1980s the Katana was the epitome of state of the art styling, ten years on it began to look tired and old-fashioned. It has, however, been discovered by a new generation and has blossomed again as a post-classic.

HONDA DREAM 300

The Dream, the first Honda to be marketed outside Japan, had a name company founder Soichiro Honda was fond of as it symbolised his ambition to conquer the world motorcycle market. The Honda Dream began as a single, but the Dream as we know it first appeared as a 250cc four-stroke twin in 1957. The C70 produced 20bhp and could reach 135kph. In 1959 the faster C75 appeared with a 305cc engine. The Dream was one of several ground-breaking Honda models that would change the face of motorcycling forever.

SUZUKI ROTARY RE5

When the RE5 first appeared late in 1974 it was treated with suspicion by many motorcyclists because of its use of a rotary engine. Germany's Felix Wankel had invented the rotary engine in the 1950s and Suzuki's engine was built with the cooperation of German motorcycle manufacturer NSU. Although the engine was smooth it was very thirsty and, at 62bhp, down on power. Suzuki gave up experimenting with the rotary at the end of 1976 but, like so many experimental bikes, it developed a cult following. Norton began developing a Wankel-engined bike in Britain around the time the RE5 was abandoned. It couldn't save Norton, but it did win the Isle of Man TT in the hands of Steve Hislop in 1992, the factory's first Senior TT victory since 1961.

SUZUKI GT750

Suzuki's two-stroke, water-cooled triple was the first and last of the big two-strokes. When it appeared in 1971 it seemed to fly in the face of industry trends. When the last one was made in 1976 the world had suffered the Middle East oil crisis, making fuel more expensive, and new emission laws were looming. Both these factors were unfavourable for two-strokes. Suzuki replaced it with the GT750, the first of the company's four-cylinder four-strokes and the forerunner of the GSX motors that have survived until today. The GT750 engine had considerable success on the race track. Geoff Perry was on his way to ride one when he died, and the British world champion Barry Sheene rode one in British and European competitions. Previous notable water-cooled two-strokes were the pre-Second World War Scott, and the Silk made from 1975 to '79.

HESKETH V1000

This machine is the vision of motor sports patron Lord Hesketh, the owner of a Formula One car racing team. Hesketh wanted to make the Aston Martin of motorcycles, a gentleman's tourer. The robust 992cc V-twin motor is basically two Westlake 500cc singles bolted together, most of the parts are sourced from quality manufacturers all over Europe and the package has been refined by Formula One engineers. The bike was plagued by one crisis after another but survived mainly through the efforts of a handful of devoted enthusiasts in the Hesketh organisation. The bike was launched in 1980 and today the small British company will still build them to order, virtually unchanged in 20 years. Only about 250 have been built, with, at last count, four in New Zealand.

SCOTT FLYING SQUIRREL 600

The brilliant Alfred Angus Scott started his motorcycle company in 1909, his first machines being made by the Jowett car firm. His 180-degree parallel two-stroke twin remained in production for almost half a century and was reinvented by the East Germans and Japanese in the 1960s. Scott engines were water-cooled from 1914. Telescopic forks began to gain popularity with manufacturers shortly before the Second World War;

Scott had them before the First World War. Rotary inlet valves provided a breakthrough for racing two-strokes in the late 1950s; Scott introduced them in 1911. He left the company in 1919 and died in 1923 but his revolutionary design work had been done. It was left to the company to continue manufacture and refine his ideas. The marque disappeared during the Second World War.

INDEX

Page numbers in italics indicate illustrations.